THE SLEEPING BEAUTY

THE SLEEPING BEAUTY

Book by Colin Wakefield

Music and Lyrics by Kate Edgar

WARNER/CHAPPELL PLAYS

LONDON

A Warner Music Group Company

THE SLEEPING BEAUTY
First published in 1996
by Warner/Chappell Plays Ltd
129 Park Street, London W1Y 3FA

ISBN 0 85676 220 2

SPECIAL NOTE ON MUSIC
The music written by Kate Edgar for THE SLEEPING BEAUTY is required for production. Please contact Warner/Chappell Plays for further information regarding the score, availability and fees.

AMATEUR PRODUCTIONS
Royalties are due at least fourteen days prior to the first performance. A royalty quotation will be issued upon receipt of the following details:

Name of Licensee
Play Title
Place of Performance
Dates and Number of Performances
Audience Capacity
Ticket Prices

PROFESSIONAL PRODUCTIONS
All enquiries regarding repertory and stock rights should be addressed to Warner/Chappell Plays Ltd, 129 Park Street, London W1Y 3FA. All other enquiries should be addressed to the authors, c/o the publisher.

OVERSEAS PRODUCTIONS
Applications for productions overseas should be addressed to our local authorized agents. Further details are listed in our catalogue of plays, published every two years, or available from Warner/Chappell Plays at the address above.

Printed by Commercial Colour Press, London E7

THE SLEEPING BEAUTY was first performed at Salisbury Playhouse on 10th December 1994, with the following cast:

KING CUTHBERT	Nigel Nobes
QUEEN ESMERALDA	Jane Karen
PRINCESS BRIAR ROSE	Emma Cunniffe
NUTS THE MONKEY	Michelle Blair
NANNY FANNY ANNIE	John Halstead
HARRY	Mark Shillabeer
L C	Raymond Sawyer
CEDRIC	Anthony Psaila
THE TIME FAIRY	Janet Rawson
PATIENCE	Michelle Blair
GRACE	Emma Cunniffe
CARABOSSE	Siân Howard
LITTLE HARRY	Brendan Chitty/Daniel Hayes

CHORUS OF PALACE CHILDREN, ATTENDANTS and BRAMBLE BOGWOPPITS played by two teams of local children (Nat Baverstock, Brendan Chitty, Charlotte Clement, David Oakes, Kimberley Rendell, Louise Rendell, Daniel Hayes, Sarah Mahoney, Catheryn Mears, Natalie Perrett, Robert Sears, Graham Sowerby).

Director	Colin Wakefield
Set designer	Norman Coates
Costume designer	Su Bentinck
Choreographer	Fran Jaynes
Fight director	Richard Ryan
Lighting designer	Peter Hunter
Sound designer	Gina Hills
On the book	Brum Gardner
Musical director/Keyboards	Simon Ashmore
Keyboards/Saxophone	Christopher Seed
Drums/Percussion	Lyn Edwards

CHARACTERS

KING CUTHBERT
QUEEN ESMERALDA
BRIAR ROSE (*their daughter — the Sleeping Beauty*)
NANNY FANNY ANNIE (*Dame*)
HARRY (*her supposed son, really* PRINCE HAL)
LORD CHANCELLOR — L C (ELSIE)
CEDRIC (*his odious son*)
NUTS (*the Princess's pet monkey*)
CARABOSSE (*the wicked fairy*)
THE TIME FAIRY (*the good fairy*)
PATIENCE (PATTI — *an American tourist fairy, Act One, Scene One only*)
GRACE (*another American tourist fairy, Act One, Scene One only*)

[NB:] PATIENCE *and* GRACE *can be played by the same actresses later playing* NUTS *and* BRIAR ROSE

CHORUS *of a minimum six children to play Palace Children, Attendants, Bramble Bogwoppits, etc, but specifically:*

GIRL ONE   BRIAR ROSE, *aged 7 (Act One, Scene Three). Small.*
GIRL TWO   *Fairly small.*
GIRL THREE   BRIAR ROSE, *aged 12 (Act One, Scene Three). Taller.*

BOY ONE   HARRY, *aged 7 (Act One, Scene One). Small.*
BOY TWO   *To match* GIRL TWO.
BOY THREE   HARRY, *aged 14 (Act One, Scene Three). Fairly tall.*

CEDRIC *as a boy (aged 12 to 14 at the beginning of the play) should be played by the adult actor throughout.*

AUTHOR'S NOTE

The pantomime was written for a cast of ten adults and six children.

The principals doubled as the Opening Chorus, and elsewhere as specified in the text. With a larger Company a separate Chorus, or whatever size, could be used for the Opening, as well as for fleshing out a number of other scenes (e.g., the arrival of the Time-o-bile and the christening through to the end of Act One, Scene One, the Spinning Wheel destruction, the celebratory ending to Act One, the chase at the end of Act Two, Scene Two, the falling asleep and awakening, and the Finale.) Similarly, more children could be used in all these scenes, and also for the marching number and the dance of the Bramble Bogwoppits.

In other words, the pantomime can be performed by ten adults and a small chorus of children, but also suits a larger company.

SCENES

ACT ONE

Scene One	Royal Hall
Scene Two	Frontcloth (outside the Castle)
Scene Three	Hedged Garden (initially behind gauze)
Scene Four	Frontcloth
Scene Five	Nanny Fanny Annie's Kitchen

ACT TWO

Scene One	Frontcloth
Scene Two	Royal Hall
Scene Three	Frontcloth
Scene Four	Tower
Scene Five	Bramble gauze
Scene Six	The overgrown Tower
Scene Seven	Frontcloth (and Songsheet)
Scene Eight	Royal Hall (Wedding and Walkdown)

NUMBERS

ACT ONE

A Christening Today	(FULL COMPANY, *ex.* NANNY)
Just the Job for Me	(NANNY)
Fairies' Blessing	(TIME FAIRY, PATIENCE, GRACE *and* COMPANY)
Time Song	(TIME FAIRY)
Adventure Duet	(BRIAR ROSE *and* HARRY)
Life is a Bowl of Cherries	(CEDRIC)
The Happiest Day of my Life	(FULL COMPANY, *ex.* TIME FAIRY *and* CARABOSSE)

ACT TWO

A Soldier's Life	(KING *and* CHILDREN)
Life is a Bowl of Cherries (reprise)	(CEDRIC)
Spinning Song	(CARABOSSE *and* BRIAR ROSE)
A Hundred Years With You	(CARABOSSE *and* TIME FAIRY)
Harry's Song	(HARRY)
Songsheet	(NANNY *and* L C)
Finale	(FULL COMPANY)

ACT ONE

Scene One

The Royal Hall.

Colourful, medieval setting. Open ceremonial hall, vista of castle turrets behind.

BRIAR ROSE'S cot stands on a small raised platform UC. Platform UR for Time-o-bile to land, and corresponding platform UL for CARABOSSE'S entrance (in this scene a spinning wheel also stands here, in the second act, the monkey's cage). Hanging (inaccessible but very prominent) above UL platform is the KING'S magic sword bearing the legend "do not steal".

Opening chorus of SERVANTS/FLUNKEYS, etc. (Actors are those later playing KING/QUEEN/HARRY/BRIAR ROSE/MONKEY/CEDRIC/ CARABOSSE/TIME FAIRY/L C and six children (quick change for LITTLE HARRY). A full company except NANNY.

Much excitement, bustle and busy good humour.

> *Number: A Christening Today (ALL)*

ALL   THE SUN IS SHINING, THE FLOWERS ALL BLOOM,
THE BIRDS ARE SINGING THEIR MERRIEST TUNE.
OUR JOBS MUST BE FINISHED WITHOUT DELAY
FOR THERE'S GOING TO BE A CHRISTENING TODAY.

SPRING IS THE LOVELIEST TIME OF THE YEAR —
SO WELCOME, FRIENDS, WHO ARE GATHERED HERE.
WE'RE ALL ARRAYED IN OUR FINEST CLOTHES
TO CELEBRATE THE CHRISTENING OF SWEET BRIAR ROSE.

FOR SEVEN LONG YEARS WE WAITED TO SEE
IF AN HEIR TO THE THRONE WAS EVER TO BE.
WE HOPED AND WE PRAYED THAT FATE WOULD BRING
A DAUGHTER OR SON FOR THE QUEEN OR THE KING.

(Instrumental and dance.)

WE'VE SCRUBBED AND WE'VE POLISHED: IT'S ALL
                      SPICK AND SPAN —
THE BIGGEST SPRING-CLEAN SINCE THE KINGDOM
                      BEGAN.
WE'RE ALL DECKED OUT IN OUR FINEST ARRAY

FOR THERE'S GOING TO BE A CHRISTENING TODAY.
WE'RE ALL ASSEMBLED, AS EVERYONE KNOWS,
TO CELEBRATE THE CHRISTENING OF SWEET BRIAR ROSE.

(*Exit the company.*)

NANNY   (*calling, off*) Harry! Harry!

(*Enter* NANNY — *on tricycle with loads of shopping. The baby*
BRIAR ROSE *may be in the tricycle basket, sporting a medieval*
crash helmet.)

NANNY   Where is that boy? Harry! Harry . . . (*Sees audience.*) Oh,
hello, dears! (*No response.*) Hello, dears! (*Hardly better.*) Of
course, you don't know me, do you? Well, I'm Fanny Annie.
Fanny Annie, the Palace Nanny. So every time I come on and
shout: "Hello, dears!" I want you all to shout back, as loud as
you can: "Hello, Nanny Fanny Annie!" Will you do that?
(*Practice, etc.*) Marvellous! I enjoyed that. I think I'll have a
drink to celebrate. (*Slug of gin:* NANNY'S *ruin.*) I've been
slaving away for days, getting everything ready for the
christening. I'm not just the Nanny, you know. Oh, no! I'm
chief cook and bottle-washer, pastry cook and dishwasher;
housemaid, nursemaid, parlourmaid and ladiesmaid;
dairymaid, chambermaid — overworked and underpaid. But
oooh — I do love a good christening. King Cuthbert and
Queen Esmeralda —they longed for a baby. Nearly gave up
hope. Then one day, out she popped — excuse my French.
She's a little poppet! Would you like to see her? (*Yes.*) Would
you? (*YES!*) And so you shall. (*She makes to go to the cot, but*
fetches the baby from the tricycle.) Here she is. Isn't she
gorgeous? They call her Briar Rose. I call her BR. B for short
and R for long. I think I'll put her back in her cot while she's
still fresh. (*She puts her to bed.*) It's going to be a big do.
They've invited some very posh godmothers. And it's going to
be a lovely day. Yesterday was so foggy you couldn't tell what
the weather was like. Seven years I've worked here — ever
since my own little boy Harry was a baby. Which reminds me
— where is he? Harry! Harr —

(*Enter* LITTLE HARRY (*Boy 1*), *aged 7, on skateboard. He*
executes an emergency stop, closely avoiding collision with
NANNY. *He carries something wrapped up in a blanket.*)

NANNY   Oooh, Harry!

HARRY   Hi, Ma!

NANNY   You naughty . . . what have you got in that blanket?

HARRY   Nuts!

NANNY   I beg your pardon! Cheeky little monkey!

HARRY   That's what it is, Ma. A little monkey. Look, a christening present for Briar Rose.

         (NANNY *looks into the blanket. We see little monkey's head.*)

NANNY   Aaaahh!

HARRY   That's its name: Nuts.

NANNY   I'll give you nuts if you don't hurry up and get ready for the christening. You could do with a good wash.

HARRY   Ma —

NANNY   You know the rules:

         Clean your teeth,
         Brush your hair —

HARRY   Change your dirty underwear.

NANNY   Scrub your feet
         Between your toes —

HARRY   Blow the bogies down your nose!

NANNY   Harry!

HARRY   All the bits you haven't done for years —

BOTH   And don't forget to wash behind your ears!

HARRY   'Bye, Ma!

         (HARRY *runs off with monkey, leaving skateboard.*)

NANNY   He's a good boy, really. And ever so fond of the baby Princess. I tell you, I was ever so lucky to get this job. I wasn't always going to be a nanny. Oh no.

         Number: Just the Job for Me (NANNY)

NANNY   ON THE DAY THAT I LEFT SCHOOL
          I DIDN'T HAVE A CLUE
          HOW I'D EARN MY LIVING —
          WHATEVER COULD I DO?

          THEN I SAW AN AD IN THE JOURNAL:
          "GO-GETTING PEOPLE REQUIRED."
          THEY ASKED ME: "CAN YOU TRAVEL?"
          I NODDED — AND I WAS HIRED.

          AND I BECAME AN ENGINE DRIVER
          ON THE 8.03 TO BATH.
          THE JOB WAS RATHER CUSHY,
          AND REALLY QUITE A LAUGH.
          THEN ONE DAY I NODDED OFF
          WHILE SITTING AT THE WHEEL.
          I MISSED THE STOP AND ONLY WOKE
          WHEN I BEGAN TO FEEL
          WATER LAPPING ROUND MY KNEES —

          IT GAVE ME QUITE A SCARE.
          I'D DRIVEN THE TRAIN ONTO THE BEACH
          AT WESTON-SUPER-MARE!

          (*spoken*) So I got the sack. I was on the breadline. Fed up
          with full-time training, I decided to do a sandwich course.
          Well, you've got to use your loaf, haven't you? I needed the
          dough, you see.

          SO I BECAME A BAKER —
          IT KEPT ME ON MY TOES.
          THE WORK WAS FUN, THE FLOUR
          KEPT GETTING UP MY NOSE.
          THEN ONE DAY IT GOT TOO MUCH:
          I LET OUT A MIGHTY SNEEZE.
          MY SET OF NEW FALSE TEETH FELL OUT —
          I GOT DOWN ON MY KNEES.
          BUT I COULDN'T FIND THEM ANYWHERE.
          NEXT DAY — I COULD HAVE DIED —
          KING CUTHBERT FOUND THEM BAKED
          INTO A LOAF OF MOTHER'S PRIDE!

          (*spoken*) So I was summoned here to the Royal Palace and set
          to work as a skivvy. Then when Briar Rose was born, the
          Queen needed a nanny. I said I'd already worked for BR, and
          got the job.

SO I BECAME THE NANNY
TO PRINCESS BRIAR ROSE.
SHE'S QUITE THE DEAREST LITTLE GIRL,
AS EVERYBODY KNOWS.
I WAKE HER IN THE MORNING —
I TUCK HER UP AT NIGHT.
AND WHEN SHE CRIES I DRY HER EYES,
MAKE SURE THAT SHE'S ALL RIGHT.
AND WHEN SHE'S LYING IN HER COT
AS SNUG AS SNUG CAN BE:
I KNOW THAT BEING A NANNY
IS JUST THE JOB FOR ME.
YOU CAN KEEP YOUR TRAINS, YOUR LOAVES OF BREAD,
IT'S HERE I WANT TO BE.
YES! BEING THE NANNY TO BRIAR ROSE
IS JUST THE JOB FOR ME!

L C   (*off*) Nanny!

NANNY   It's the Lord Chancellor.

L C   (*entering*) Nanny!

NANNY   Isn't he gorgeous!

L C   Nann — (*He slips on the skateboard. Pratfall.*) Aaaarrrhhh!

NANNY   Oooops! Are you alright, dear?

L C   (*recovering*) No, I'm not alright.

NANNY   Sorry, Elsie.

L C   And don't call me Elsie.

NANNY   But that's your name. (*Pointing to the large initials on his costume.*) El-sie.

L C   Those are my initials, you fool. L C: the Lord Chancellor.

NANNY   Elsie, the Lord Chancellor!

L C   Doh! Can't you spell?

NANNY   I spell very well. I went to school you know, Elsie. I learnt the three R's.

L C   Reading, writing and arithmetic?

NANNY   No: reading, writing and rotten.

L C   What was rotten?

NANNY   My reading and writing.

L C   Doh! You should hurry up. You'll be late for the christening.

NANNY   I had a lot to do today, Elsie. (*Bending over to pick up the skateboard.*) I've got a little behind.

L C   That's a matter of opinion.

NANNY   Ooooh — you saucy!

             (*Enter* CEDRIC.)

CEDRIC   *I'm* ready for the christening, father.

L C   You see — Cedric's ready, aren't you, Cedric?

CEDRIC   Yes, father — I'm ready.

NANNY   Yuk!

L C   What?

CEDRIC   She's got my skateboard!

NANNY   No I haven't, dear. This is Harry's skateboard.

CEDRIC   (*tantrum*) It's mine! It's mine! It's mine!

NANNY   Oooh! You little fibber!

CEDRIC   I hate you!

NANNY   It is Harry's skateboard. (*To audience.*) Isn't it?

AUDIENCE   YES!

CEDRIC   Oh no it isn't!

AUD/NANNY   Oh yes it is!

             (*This three times, with* L C *joining* CEDRIC.)

L C	Oh. Very well then, it is. But I'm confiscating it anyway. Cedric — you can have it.
CEDRIC	Thank you, father. (*He puts his tongue out at* NANNY.)
NANNY	Horrid little brat!
L C	What?
NANNY	Gosh, is that . . . the time? Must dash. 'Bye, everyone!
AUDIENCE	Bye!

(*Exit* NANNY, *on tricycle.*)

L C	Now remember, Cedric — be polite to Queen Esmeralda.
CEDRIC	But she's so bossy.
L C	And to King Cuthbert.
CEDRIC	He's plain daft!

(*Enter two* PAGES (*Boys 2 and 3*) *with trumpets, and* FLUNKEY (*actor playing* ADULT HARRY.) *Fanfare.*)

FLUNKEY	Pray silence for their most excellent excellencies, King Cuthbert and Queen Esmeralda.

(*Enter* KING CUTHBERT *with kitchen mop as hobby horse, with toy sword and dustbin lid as shield.*)

KING	Charge!

(*He gallops round the stage, neighing etc.* L C *and* CEDRIC *scatter. Enter* QUEEN ESMERALDA, *also at a gallop.*)

QUEEN	Charge!!
KING	(*continuing*) Charge!!

(*They almost bump into each other.* KING *neighs.*)

QUEEN	I'm not playing any more. Cuthbert — give Elsie your sword.
KING	Yes, dear.

QUEEN   And your shield.

KING   Yes, dear.

QUEEN   And your horse.

KING   Oh no — not Horsie!

QUEEN   *And* your horse.

KING   Yes, dear.

            (*He hands over each, as ordered, to* L C *who passes them immediately to* CEDRIC.)

QUEEN   Elsie — what's the time?

L C   Time for the christening, your majesty.

QUEEN   Then call the archbishop.

L C   This instant, your majesty. Come along, Cedric.

CEDRIC   (*bowing and grovelling*) Excuse us, your most majestical impressivenesses.

            (*Exit* L C *and* CEDRIC.)

QUEEN   What a polite young man.

KING   He's a creep! (*Crying from the cot.*)

QUEEN   Now you've woken the baby.

            (*She takes* BRIAR ROSE *from the cot.*)

KING   You were making all the noise.

QUEEN   (*getting louder, as does crying*) No I wasn't!

KING   Yes you were!

QUEEN   Wasn't!

KING   Were!

QUEEN   Were!

KING	Wasn't! Doh!
QUEEN	You take her, then. She's all damp and smelly!

(*She hands the baby to* KING.)

KING	Yuk! Maybe she needs a new nappy.
QUEEN	Don't be silly. She had a new one yesterday!
KING	Nanny will know what to do.
QUEEN	Nanny!
KING	Nanny!
BOTH	Nanny!

(*Enter* NANNY.)

NANNY	(*to audience*) Hello, dears!
AUDIENCE	Hello, Nanny Fanny Annie! (*Audience may need a refresher.*)
NANNY	How's my little Briar Rosie-posie?
QUEEN	Rather whiffy, Nanny!
KING	A bit sniffy, frankly!
NANNY	Oooh! Who's done a doo-doo pooh-pooh!
QUEEN	Phew!
KING	What a pong!
NANNY	Pappy unhappy — nappy crappy.
KING/QUEEN	Nanny!
NANNY	Leave her to me, dears. I won't be a jiffy. (*To audience.*) 'Bye!

(*Exit* NANNY *with* BRIAR ROSE.)

KING	This baby business is greatly overrated, if you ask me. What do we need a christening for, anyway? I'd much rather be out having a good battle. Biff, boff, bang, slam —

QUEEN   Be quiet, Cuthbert. The Fairy Godmothers will be here in a minute. I hope you remembered to invite everyone.

KING   I left all that to Elsie. I say, when do you think she'll be old enough for her first suit of armour?

QUEEN   Briar Rose?

KING   I've seen some excellent new chain mail for 25p a yard.

QUEEN   (*far too expensive*) 25p!

KING   It is first class mail!

QUEEN   Cuthbert — I am not having our daughter fighting battles, chain mail or no chain mail. Anyway, there's nobody left to fight since you defeated that nice King Henry next door and stole his kingdom.

KING   Brilliant battle, that! Biff, boff, bang!

QUEEN   Be quiet, Cuthbert! It was quite revolting. You know I hate falling out with the neighbours.

KING   I captured his magic sword, didn't I?

QUEEN   Magic, my foot! What good's it ever done us?

KING   We had a baby, didn't we?

QUEEN   Seven years later! I wonder what happened to King Henry's baby son, that dear little Prince Hal —

KING   *Don't mention the Prince*!

QUEEN   There'll be trouble if he turns up one day wanting his kingdom back.

KING   There certainly will: I'll have his head chopped off for starters. It's ages since we had a good execution.

     (*Enter* L C, *dressed extravagantly as archbishop.*)

L C   Your majesty.

KING   Elsie! What are you doing in that funny hat?

L C   I am the archbishop, your majesty.

KING   Don't be silly. Archbishops are much older than that.

L C   ·   Oh, sorry. (*Very old voice.*) I am the archbishop, your
                    majesty.

                    (*Sound of Time-o-bile arriving.*)

QUEEN   Cuthbert, what's that noise?

KING   Probably just an invasion.

                    (*The Time-o-bile begins to descend — flashing lights at
                    bottom. Smoke for landing.*)

KING   (*realisation*) Invasion! Help! Don't panic! Nanny! Elsie!
                    Invasion! Help!

                    (*Enter* NANNY, LITTLE HARRY (*still with monkey*) CEDRIC *and
                    three Girls. The Time-o-bile lands.*)

KING   (*continuing*) Elsie! Help! Invasion!

                    (*Flash.* TIME FAIRY *enters from the Time-o-bile, followed by*
                    PATIENCE *and* GRACE — *as American attendants.*)

TIME FAIRY   Don't panic! It's me — not an invasion.
             The Time Fairy. Got your kind invitation.
             Heard you needed some Godmothers today.
             Christening is it? We've come a long way.
             Lightning-fast in my Time-o-bile I fly —
             From future to past, in the blink of an eye.
             Let me introduce my assistants here:
             I met them in the States early next year:
             Patience —

                    (PATIENCE *and* GRACE *come down from the landing platform.*)

PATIENCE   Call me Patti! Hi!

GRACE   And I'm Grace.
             Hey, this is wild! I just love this place!
             Dig that spinning wheel.

PATIENCE   And what a cute Princess!
             Early to mid-Cuthbertian, I guess.

TIME FAIRY   We've come to bring her blessings galore.

KING   We're honoured.

QUEEN   You're all most welcome, I'm sure.

             Number: Fairies' Blessing (TIME FAIRY/PATTI/GRACE)

TIME FAIRY   WHEN A CHILD IS BORN
             YOU HOPE AND PRAY
             THAT AS SHE GROWS
             EVERYDAY
             WILL SEE HER SAFE
             AND FREE FROM FEAR.
             SO THAT IS WHY
             WE'LL BE NEAR.

TRIO   WE'LL BE WITH YOU,
             GUIDING YOU ON YOUR WAY.
             WE'LL BE WITH YOU,
             LENDING A HELPING HAND EACH DAY.
             THOUGH YOU CAN'T SEE US
             WE'LL BE THERE —

PATTI   REMINDING YOU TO BRUSH YOUR HAIR.

TIME FAIRY   KEEPING YOU SAFE AND SOUND —
TRIO   WE'LL BE AROUND.

TRIO   WE'LL BE WITH YOU,
             WATCHING YOU AS YOU GROW.
             WE'LL BE WITH YOU,
             GUIDING YOUR FOOTSTEPS AS YOU GO.
             WE'LL PROTECT YOU WHILE YOU SLEEP

GRACE   AND MAKE SURE YOU ALWAYS CLEAN YOUR TEETH.
TRIO   KEEPING YOU SAFE AND SOUND —
             WE'LL BE AROUND.

TIME FAIRY   WE'LL DRY HER TEARS IF SHE SCRAPES HER KNEES,
             HELP HER REVISE FOR HER GCSE'S.
             SEE HER SAFE ON HER VERY FIRST DATE,

PATTI/GRACE BUT ONLY IF SHE DON'T STAY OUT TOO LATE.

TIME FAIRY   WE'LL NURSE HER THROUGH THE CHICKEN POX,
             CHECK SHE REMEMBERS TO CHANGE HER SOCKS.

TRIO	WE'LL EVEN DO OUR VERY BEST TO SEE SHE PASSES HER DRIVING TEST! SHE'LL BE KIND, SHE'LL HE FAIR. SHE'LL BE SAFE IN THE DRAGON'S LAIR.
PATTI	SHE'LL BE MERRY,
GRACE	SHE'LL BE BRAVE.
PATTI/GRACE	SHE'LL BE LIVELY,
TIME FAIRY	SHE'LL BEHAVE!
TRIO	SHE'LL BE HAPPY, SHE'LL DANCE AND SING. SHE'LL BE A CREDIT TO THE QUEEN AND KING. (*very quiet*) WE'LL BE WITH YOU . . .
L C	(*spoken*) I christen this child . . .
KING	(*prompting*) Briar Rose.
TRIO	(*very quiet*) WE'LL BE WITH YOU . . .
L C	*Brian Toes!*
QUEEN	Briar Rose!
TRIO	(*very quiet*) WE'LL BE WITH YOU . . .
L C	I christen this child Briar Rose.
ALL	WE'LL BE WITH YOU, GUIDING YOU ON YOUR WAY. WE'LL BE WITH YOU, LENDING A HELPING HAND EACH DAY.
TRIO	THOUGH YOU CAN'T SEE US, WE'LL BE NEAR, SO YOU CAN GROW UP FREE FROM FEAR. KEEPING YOU SAFE AND SOUND, WE'LL BE AROUND.
ALL	(*except* TRIO) WE'LL BE AROUND.
ALL	WE'LL BE AROUND.

(*Flash. Enter* CARABOSSE. *Thunder, lightning.* GIRLS *scream and flee.*)

CARABOSSE   I, Carabosse, interrupt this christening —
Cross and indignant: you'd better be listening!
I come to demand an explanation:
Why did I receive no invitation?

KING   Well . . .

QUEEN   We thought . . .

L C   Since you're such a recluse —

CARABOSSE   I've never heard such a feeble excuse!
Spurned, uninvited — that's always my fate.
Well, it's time *you* learned the meaning of hate.
The object of my loathing — Briar Rose.
I hate that baby more than you suppose.

QUEEN   We're sorry!

TIME FAIRY   They'll make amends!

CARABOSSE   How?

KING   Tell us!

CARABOSSE   Too late!

NANNY   I reckon the old cow's jealous!

CARABOSSE   Powers of Darkness — do your worst!
Harken to Carabosse's curse:
Happy for sixteen years this brat will be —
Healthy and strong: anathema to me!
Short-lived her happiness — Time will fly.
Heed my prediction, for I tell no lie.
On her sixteenth birthday the apple of your eye
Will prick her finger on a spinning wheel — and DIE!

(*Thunder, lightning. Exit* CARABOSSE.)

QUEEN   Cuthbert — don't just stand there! Say something!

KING   Righto!

QUEEN   Do something!

KING   Righto!

QUEEN   Is that all you can say?

KING   Yes.

QUEEN   Why?

KING   You're standing on my right toe!

QUEEN   Pah!

KING   Elsie, do something!

L C   Righto!

KING   Watchit!

CEDRIC   *I've* got an idea.

QUEEN   What?

CEDRIC   That nasty witch said that Briar Rose would prick her finger, right?

QUEEN   Right.

CEDRIC   On a spinning wheel, right?

KING/QUEEN Right.

CEDRIC   (*with relish*) And die, right?

K/Q/L C   Right.

CEDRIC   Well — if we chopped all Briar Rose's fingers off she wouldn't be able to prick any of them on a spinning wheel, would she?

L C   Right!

KING   Right!

QUEEN   Wrong! Fool! (*Strikes* KING *on the arm.*)

KING   Wrong! Fool! (*Strikes* L C *on the arm.*)

L C   Wrong! Fool! (*Strikes* CEDRIC *on the arm.*)

CEDRIC   Wrong! Fool! (*Hits* LITTLE HARRY *over the head.*)

HARRY   Aaarrrhhh!

NANNY   Don't you hit my boy!

QUEEN   Nanny — don't interfere!

             (HARRY *stamps on* CEDRIC'S *foot. The following speeches build
             and overlap. Others on stage can ad lib once the main
             speeches are established and the cacophony increases. All
             stop on* TIME FAIRY'S *interruption.*)

QUEEN   And what's that wretched child of yours doing here anyway?
             Is anybody listening to me? Cuthbert — will you stop
             snivelling and do something! Standing around there like a
             damp face flannel. Cuthbert! Cuthbert! Are you listening to
             me? (*Etc.*)

NANNY   I'll interfere if I want to. Wretched child, indeed! (*To*
             CEDRIC.) Well, you deserved it. I don't care if you are the Lord
             Chancellor's son, you snivelling little snot-face. I hope it
             hurt. (*Etc.*)

L C   He'll hit your miserable infant if he wants to, you interfering
             old bat! (*To* KING.) You told me not to invite Carabosse, your
             majesticality. (*To* NANNY.) How dare you address the son of
             the Lord Chancellor in that tone of voice! (*Etc.*)

KING   Why wasn't Carabosse invited, anyway? I'll have your head
             chopped off for this! My poor, darling Briar Rose! Who'll
             fight my battles now after I'm dead and gone? Yes, alright
             dear — I'm listening. (*Etc.*)

CEDRIC   Aaarrhhh! He hit me, father! He stamped on my foot! It was a
             jolly good idea of mine, anyway: she can't prick her finger if
             all her fingers have already gone. I'll chop them off myself if
             you want. (*Etc.*)

             (*The* TIME FAIRY *interrupts. All stop.*)

TIME FAIRY   Quiet! Stop squabbling! Fighting's a crime
             At a moment like this — a total waste of Time.
             I am cleverer than Carabosse, so
             I have the power to soften the blow.
             The Princess, aged sixteen, I can reveal

Will prick her finger on a spinning wheel,
But will not die. To allay your fears:
She will simply sleep for one hundred years.
The sweetest of dreams I can guarantee.
For her peace and safety — just count on me.
Fast asleep — like a little chrysalis:
To be woken at last by a Prince — with a kiss!
My word — is that the time? We have to fly!

GRACE   Due back in the States.

PATIENCE   For the Fourth of July.

(*Both get into the Time-o-bile.*)

TIME FAIRY   I'm so busy nowadays, I could cry!

GRACE   Thanks for the invite!

PATIENCE   See ya!

(TIME FAIRY *gets on board.*)

ALL THREE   Cheeri-bye!

(*They wave. Door closes. Take-off. Smoke and flashing lights.
Company call their goodbyes.* CEDRIC, L C, NANNY *and*
FLUNKEY *stay upstage. Frontcloth in, behind* KING, QUEEN *and*
LITTLE HARRY.)

                         Scene Two

Castle frontcloth.

KING, QUEEN *and* LITTLE HARRY *remain.*

KING   Well, that's alright then. Briar Rose won't have to die after
             all.

QUEEN   It's not alright, you bumbling buffoon. By the time Briar Rose
             wakes up after her hundred-year lie-in, how old do you think
             we'll be?

KING   About 140?

QUEEN	Exactly, bird-brain. We'll be long gone. Even that wretched urchin will be over 100 . . . (*To* HARRY.) What have you got there?
HARRY	A present for the Princess, your majesty.
QUEEN	Ugh! It's a monkey! Take it away. It'll be riddled with fleas!

(HARRY *exits quickly*.)

This is all your fault, Cuthbert, for not inviting Carabosse to the christening.

KING	That was Elsie's fault.
QUEEN	Anyway, Briar Rose will never wake up.
KING	She will. She's going to be kissed by a Prince. That nice Time Fairy said so.
QUEEN	And where's this famous Prince going to come from, bungle-bonce? They don't grow on trees, you know.
KING	They grow on family trees. (*Joke.*) Family trees!
QUEEN	Cuthbert! If that nice Prince Hal still lived next door . . .
KING	*Don't mention the Prince!*

(*Enter* NANNY.)

NANNY	We'd all be a lot better off if you two stopped quarrelling.
KING	Nonsense. If we stopped quarrelling, nothing would ever get done.
QUEEN	Yes, it would!
KING	No, it wouldn't!
QUEEN	Would!
KING	Wouldn't!
QUEEN	Wouldn't!
KING	Would! Doh!

NANNY   You're barmy!

QUEEN   Nanny!

NANNY   Both of you!

KING   How dare you!

QUEEN   Back to the kitchen!

NANNY   (*going*) Stark staring bonkers!

KING   I didn't come here to be insulted.

NANNY   Really? Where do you usually go?

            (*Exit* NANNY.)

KING   Doh!

            (*Enter* L C.)

L C   Your majesty . . .

KING   (*impatient*) What is it?

L C   I've thought of a plan.

KING   What sort of plan?

L C   If we destroyed all the spinning wheels in the kingdom —
            then the Princess won't be able to prick her finger on any of
            them. Brilliant, don't you think?

KING   Er . . .

QUEEN   Ridiculous!

KING   Ridiculous!

L C   (*calling*) Cedric! Bring on the Spinning Wheel Destruction
            Machine!

            (CEDRIC *wheels on the machine, which should open out into a
            Heath Robinson contraption, with smoke, flashing lights etc.
            It might be placed over a trap, so as to seem to eat more than
            its apparent capacity.*)

L C   Open it up!

CEDRIC   Yes, father.

               (*He opens up the machine.*)

KING   I say!

L C   I've penned you a proclamation, your majesticality.

               (*He hands over a long scroll to the* KING, *who reads.*)

KING   I, King Cuthbert, proclaim throughout the land
               That from today all spinning wheels are banned.
               If you own one — go and get it.
               Hand it in or you'll regret it.
               Suffer death or painful torture —
               This is done to save my dorture! Er . . . daughter!

QUEEN   It'll never work.

               (*Enter* NANNY, *with a spinning wheel.*)

NANNY   Hello, dears!

AUDIENCE   Hello, Nanny Fanny Annie!

L C   It's working already.

NANNY   (*to* QUEEN) Here you are, dear.

QUEEN   (*to* KING) Here you are, dear.

KING   (*to* CEDRIC) Here you are, dear.

CEDRIC   Put it in!

               (KING *feeds the wheel into the machine.* CEDRIC *turns the
               handle. Munching and gurgling, followed by a loud burp.*)

NANNY   I'd like to say this is the best idea you've ever had.

KING   Thank you, Nanny!

NANNY   (*aside*) I'd like to, but I can't!

KING   Nanny! Elsie! Search the kingdom! (NANNY *and* L C *go down
               into the auditorium: ad-lib searching.*) Roll up! Look sharp!

Hand in your spinning wheels here! (*Girl brings on small wheel which* CEDRIC *feeds into the machine.*) Save a Princess today! Any more for any more! (*Another wheel handed up from pit and put in machine.*)

QUEEN   Thank you, Maestro! Much obliged!

(KING *may continue as necessary, then* NANNY *stops at a given seat, under which a box has been planted.*)

NANNY   Aha! Excuse me, your majesticals!

KING   What is it, Nanny?

NANNY   A spinning wheel, your majesticals! Under this person's seat!

L C   (*joining* NANNY) Under that person's seat!

NANNY   (*producing box*) "The Acme Wheel Construction Kit — A Winner Spinner." Oooh!

QUEEN   He's (she's) a traitor!

KING   Traitor! Stand up!

(*Audience member stands up.*)

KING   Did you or did you not hide that spinning wheel under your seat?

VICTIM   No!

KING   Do you promise?

VICTIM   Yes!

KING   All right. I believe you. I'm in a very good mood today. Those construction kits never work, anyway. Come on, let's get rid of it. (L C *hands up the box, which is destroyed in the machine.*) Is that the last one?

NANNY   Yes, your majesticals.

KING   Very well. Take away the remains and burn them.

(*Exit* CEDRIC *with the machine.* NANNY *returns to the stage.*)

NANNY   Come on Elsie. Let me light *your* fire!

(*Exit* NANNY *with* L C.)

QUEEN   Cuthbert — I'm proud of you! You can have as many battles
           as you like!

KING   Thank you, dearest.

           (*She kisses him.*)

           Doh!

           (*Exit* QUEEN.)

           So much for Carabosse's spell —
           Thanks to Cuthbert — all is well.
           Briar Rose will neither sleep nor die —
           Oh, what a clever, clever King am I!

           (*Exit* KING. *Frontcloth out, a gauze behind.*)

                         Scene Three

Hedged Garden. (*Behind gauze.*)

*Arches at centre back and at either side of rectangular hedged area.
Perhaps ornamental rose trees either side of central bench.*

Gauze, frontlit initially, with a rose garden effect.

Enter TIME FAIRY, *as* KING *exits from Scene Two.*

TIME FAIRY Less clever, I have to say, than he might suppose.
            Nevertheless, day by day, little Briar Rose
            Over sixteen years will thrive. You've heard how Time flies:
            So watch her grow before your very eyes.

            (*Courtyard lit behind gauze after start of song. First tableau
            discovered.* (*For precise stages, see after song.*) TIME FAIRY
            *remains in front and to side of gauze — and "presides" over
            the growing-up sequence in song.*)

            Number: Time Song (TIME FAIRY)

TIME FAIRY AS THE HANDS OF THE CLOCK
            GO TICK TICK TOCK,
            AND THE BALMY BREEZES BLOW —

LIKE A SPINNING TOP
THAT WILL NEVER STOP,
SO THE CHILDREN START TO GROW.
SO COME WITH ME AND STAY,   (A)
AS WE WATCH THE CHILDREN PLAY.

Instrumental.   (B)

AND AS THE DAYS GO BY,
AND THE WEEKS GO BY,
EVERYBODY KNOWS
THAT THE HAPPIEST CHILD IN THE KINGDOM
IS PRINCESS BRIAR ROSE.   (C)

AS THE HANDS OF THE CLOCK
GO TICK TICK TOCK,
AND THE TREES REACH TO THE SKY —
SO THE CHILDREN ALL   (D)
GROW STRONG AND TALL,
AS THE YEARS PASS QUICKLY BY.
SO COME WITH ME AND STAY,
AS WE WATCH THE CHILDREN PLAY.

Instrumental x2   (E)

AND AS THE MONTHS GO BY,
AND THE YEARS GO BY,
EVERYBODY KNOWS
THAT THE MERRIEST MAID IN THE KINGDOM
IS PRINCESS BRIAR ROSE.

(*Suggested sequence during Time Song as follows. Each
section should merge easily into the next — in dumbshow —
during the number.*)

(A)   *Bleed through gauze: Tableau.* NANNY *seated, maybe with
        embroidery.* BRIAR ROSE (*aged* 7: GIRL 1) *being given piggy
        back by* HARRY (*aged* 14: BOY 3).

(B)   *Tableau comes alive. Children run around,* BRIAR ROSE *waving
        to* NANNY. NUTS *joins. They play tag.*

(C)   BRIAR ROSE *and* HARRY *run off. We see them passing behind
        back arch.* NANNY *stays, then goes off to look for them.*

(D)   BRIAR ROSE (*aged* 12: GIRL 3) *appears from opposite arch,
        chased by* NUTS. (*No* HARRY *in this section.*) KING *and* QUEEN
        enter. BRIAR ROSE *curtseys, and exits with them. Again, we see*

them going behind back arch. NUTS, *who hid behind bush when* QUEEN *entered, swings on rail behind bench.*

(E)   *During second instrumental,* ADULT BRIAR ROSE *and* ADULT HARRY *join* NUTS, *and play. Freeze on* TIME FAIRY'S *'pause' below. Music stops on her 'cut'.*

TIME FAIRY   It's Time to press 'PAUSE' — Time to call 'CUT!'
The Princess is blithe and high-spirited — BUT:
(*Gauze rises over the following couplet.*)
She's nearly sixteen — I thought you should know:
Her birthday is looming — three days to go.

(TIME FAIRY *unfreezes them and exits.*)

HARRY   What do you want for your birthday, Princess?

BRIAR ROSE   Nothing, Harry. You can't afford it.

HARRY   But sixteen's special.

BRIAR ROSE   You're telling me! I can't wait! I've never left this boring old castle in my whole life. The King and Queen won't let me — I've no idea why. But after I'm sixteen they've promised I can go wherever I like!

HARRY   I'll miss you.

BRIAR ROSE   You can always come with me. And Nuts, of course.

(*Enter* NANNY.)

NANNY   Hello, dears!

AUDIENCE   Hello, Nanny Fanny Annie!

NANNY   I've just been baking, dears. Here you are. A nutty bun for Nuts. (*Excitement from* NUTS.) And a jam tart and a doughnut for you two. (*She gives both to* HARRY.)

HARRY   Thanks, Ma!

BRIAR ROSE   Thank you, Nanny.

NANNY   Must dash, dears. I haven't even started your birthday cake yet.

(*Exit* NANNY.)

HARRY	Which to you want, Princess? The doughnut or the jam tart?
BRIAR ROSE	I don't mind. Look — I wish you wouldn't call me 'Princess' all the time.
HARRY	The King said he'd chop my head off if I called you Briar Rose again. He says I'm getting too familiar.

(*Enter* CEDRIC.)

CEDRIC	Princess Briar Rose — the Queen wants to see you. Now.
BRIAR ROSE	Bother! Harry — save me one of those till I get back. I don't mind which.

(*Exit* BRIAR ROSE.)

CEDRIC	One of what?
HARRY	Mind your own business!
CEDRIC	Watchit! I'm the Lord Chancellor's son, I am. What have you got?
HARRY	A doughnut and a jam tart.
CEDRIC	Give me one!
HARRY	No!
CEDRIC	Go on!
HARRY	No!
CEDRIC	I'll pay for it — 10p.
HARRY	Alright. You can have mine. 10p — agreed?
CEDRIC	Agreed.
HARRY	Which do you want?
CEDRIC	The doughnut.
HARRY	OK. (*He gives* CEDRIC *the doughnut.*) 10p, please.
CEDRIC	I've changed my mind. I'll have the jam tart.

HARRY   OK. Have the jam tart. (*He gives* CEDRIC *the jam tart.*)

CEDRIC   There's your doughnut. (*He gives back the doughnut.*)

HARRY   Thanks.

CEDRIC   (*exiting*) See ya!

HARRY   Hey! Come back! You haven't paid me for the jam tart! 10p
             — we agreed!

CEDRIC   I gave you the doughnut!

HARRY   But you didn't pay for that either.

CEDRIC   Of course not! I didn't eat it! I'm not paying for something I
             didn't eat. Ta-ra!

             (*Exit* CEDRIC.)

HARRY   Hey! Come back!

             (*Re-enter* BRIAR ROSE.)

BRIAR ROSE   The Queen didn't want to see me at all. That vile Cedric was
             playing tricks again.

HARRY   That vile Cedric has just cheated me of 10p.

BRIAR ROSE   I'll get it back for you. Watch. Cedric! Cedric!

             (*Re-enter* CEDRIC.)

CEDRIC   Watcha want?

BRIAR ROSE   I bet you 10p you can't say 'doughnuts' every time I ask a
             question.

CEDRIC   Bet you I can!

BRIAR ROSE   Right — get out your 10p.

CEDRIC   OK.

BRIAR ROSE   Remember: you have to say 'doughnuts' every time I ask a
             question.

CEDRIC   Right.

BRIAR ROSE   Are you ready?

CEDRIC   Yes. (*Gong.*)

BRIAR ROSE   Aha! You didn't say 'doughnuts'.

CEDRIC   That's not fair. I didn't know you'd started.

BRIAR ROSE   Alright, I'll let you off. Try it again.

CEDRIC   Right.

BRIAR ROSE   Ready?

CEDRIC   Doughnuts!

BRIAR ROSE   That wasn't very difficult, was it?

CEDRIC   No. (*Gong.*)

BRIAR ROSE   Aha! Caught you again!

CEDRIC   That's not fair.

BRIAR ROSE   Alright — one last time. Ready?

CEDRIC   Doughnuts!

BRIAR ROSE   Got it right then, didn't you?

CEDRIC   Doughnuts!

BRIAR ROSE   Which would you rather have — 10p or doughnuts?

CEDRIC   Doughnuts!

BRIAR ROSE   Then I'll have the 10p. (*She takes it.*)

CEDRIC   Hey! You cheat!

HARRY   Takes one to know one.

CEDRIC   I'll get you Harry. Just you wait.

BRIAR ROSE   Here's your doughnut, Cedric.

CEDRIC   (*gritted teeth*) Thank you.

                (BRIAR ROSE *throws it to him.* NUTS *intercepts.*)

CEDRIC   Hey you, Nuts! Come back!

                (*Exit* CEDRIC, *chasing* NUTS.)

BRIAR ROSE   I wish you weren't so poor, Harry.

HARRY   I'm alright.

BRIAR ROSE   I think I'd go mad here if it wasn't for you. Kept in all the
                time — I'm so bored. I tell you, Harry — I'm planning such
                adventures.

                Number: Adventure Duet (BRIAR ROSE/HARRY.)

BRIAR ROSE   I WANT TO GO ON SAFARI IN AFRICA,
                BACK-PACK THROUGH NEPAL;
                ROW ACROSS THE ATLANTIC,
                FIGHT TIGERS IN BENGAL.

                THEN I'LL CLIMB MOUNT EVEREST,
                PADDLE UP THE NILE;
                FISH FOR SHARKS IN A BLUE LAGOON,
                CAPTURE A CROCODILE.

HARRY   A CROCODILE?!

BRIAR ROSE   CROCODILE DUNDEE
                WILL HAVE NOTHING ON ME!

                THERE ARE SO MANY PLACES IN THE WORLD —
                THINGS TO SEE AND DO.
                LET'S VISIT THEM TOGETHER —
                ME AND YOU.

HARRY   ME?

BRIAR ROSE   (*spoken*) Yes, Harry. What adventures do you want?

HARRY   Well . . .

                I WANT TO CAPTAIN A PIRATE SHIP
                AND SAIL THE SEVEN SEAS.
                I'D ROAM THE OCEANS OF THE WORLD,
                DOING AS I PLEASE.

I'D COMMANDEER A CLIPPER
AND TAKE HER FOR A SPIN;
CAPTURE A SPANISH GALLEON —
LOOK OUT, ERROL FLYNN!

BRIAR ROSE   ERROL FLYNN?!

HARRY   JUST LIKE ERROL FLYNN
             I'LL ALWAYS WIN!

SPLIT   LET'S PACK OUR BAGS,
             BOOK THE TICKET —
             THUMB A LIFT,
             TAKE THE TRAIN.
             RIDE A CAMEL,
             OR A HORSE —
             CATCH THE BUS,
             OR AN AEROPLANE.
             LET'S GO!

BOTH   WE'LL SAIL ACROSS THE OCEAN,
             TRAVEL FAR AND WIDE;
             HITCH A LIFT ON A SHOOTING STAR,
             TAKE A MAGIC CARPET RIDE.
             CATCH A ROCKET TO THE MOON,
             SEE VENUS JUST FOR FUN;
             THEN SKIM ACROSS THE MILKY WAY —
             AND ON TOWARDS THE SUN.

             THERE ARE SEVEN WONDERS OF THE WORLD,
             A THOUSAND SIGHTS TO SEE.
             LET'S VISIT THEM TOGETHER —
             YOU AND ME.

             THERE ARE SO MANY PLACES IN THE WORLD,
             THINGS TO SEE AND DO.
             IT'S TIME FOR AN ADVENTURE —
             ME AND YOU.
             ME AND YOU!

             (*Frontcloth in.*)

                              Scene Four

Frontcloth.

A flash. Enter CARABOSSE.

CARABOSSE   It's me again. Ooh — I'm so excited.
            They'll soon regret I wasn't invited!
            In three days' time — at last! — I shall have won.
            The Princess will die. Let Justice be done!

            (*Enter* TIME FAIRY.)

TIME FAIRY Won, my foot! Did you really think, you creep,
            That I'd let Briar Rose die? She will sleep
            For a hundred years. I've arranged all this,
            With a wedding to follow: perfect bliss!

CARABOSSE   A happy ending? Yuk!

TIME FAIRY   Admit defeat!
            You know that your powers are incomplete.

CARABOSSE   Too bad! You've left out of your reckoning
            The magic sword belonging to the King.

TIME FAIRY What of it?

CARABOSSE   I intend to make it mine.
            Then I'll have the power I need — divine!
            I've made plans —

TIME FAIRY   They'd better be clever.
            The King would never, I repeat 'never',
            Give up his magic sword. And if he should —
            Owning it wouldn't do *you* any good!

CARABOSSE   You lie!

TIME FAIRY   That sword was stolen by the King
            And is as useless as a piece of string
            To him, or you, or any other thief.

CARABOSSE   Then why's it magic — clever?

TIME FAIRY   Oh — good grief!
            Don't you *ever* use your brain? Only the heir
            To King Henry the Good — Prince Hal the Fair —
            Can revive its magic powers — so there!

CARABOSSE   What utter rot! I don't believe a word!
            I need that magic sword —

TIME FAIRY	Don't be absurd!

CARABOSSE   Then I shall reign supreme —

TIME FAIRY   Well, you can try.

CARABOSSE   Darkness and despair: the Princess *will* die!

(*Exit* CARABOSSE.)

TIME FAIRY   She's so bitter, you know — I can't think why!

(*Digital sound.*) Beep beep. (*x5 — as iambic pentameter.*)

My word — Is that the time? Or am I fast?
Must fly: a quick trip into the past!
Can't remember why. Oh yes: Asia Minor —
Grand opening: the Great Wall of China.
Back in time for Briar Rose's birthday
In three days precisely: don't go away.

(*Exit* TIME FAIRY. *Enter* KING — *broom for a horse, colander as a helmet and loofah as a truncheon. He canters across the stage.*)

KING   Charge!

QUEEN   (*off*) Cuthbert!

KING   (*continuing*) Charge!

(*Enter* QUEEN.)

QUEEN   Cuthbert! (*He stops: neigh.*) No battle practice today. (*She hits him on his helmet with the loofah.*)

KING   It's not fair. I haven't had a decent battle for ages.

QUEEN   Cuthbert! In three days' time Briar Rose will be sixteen.

KING   So?

QUEEN   So what do we do on a Princess's sixteenth birthday?

KING   Sing Happy Birthday?

QUEEN   Yes, and what else?

KING   Have a birthday cake?

QUEEN   And what else?

KING   Er . . . we could have sixteen executions to celebrate.

QUEEN   We marry her off, bacon-bonce. (*She hits him again.*)

KING   Marry her off? She's far too young to get married. It would be
            a disaster.

QUEEN   I married you when I was sixteen.

KING   (*removing his helmet*) I rest my case!

QUEEN   Huh! (*She hits him again. Pratfall.*)

KING   Who would she marry, anyway? There aren't any Princes left.

QUEEN   She can marry Cedric!

KING   (*appalled*) Cedric!

QUEEN   Cedric!

            (*Enter* CEDRIC.)

CEDRIC   Hello!

KING   That wimp?

CEDRIC   Eh?

QUEEN   Cedric, dear: we propose to marry you.

CEDRIC   Wot? Both of ya?

QUEEN   To Briar Rose.

CEDRIC   Uh?

QUEEN   Lost for words! What a poppet! Come along, Cuthbert. Let's
            go and tell Elsie the good news.

KING   I flatly refuse to give my consent.

QUEEN   I'll let you play with your magic sword.

KING   Promise?

QUEEN   Yes.

KING   Agreed!

QUEEN   Come along, then.

KING   Yes, dear.

                (*Exit* KING *and* QUEEN.)

CEDRIC   Married! Yuk! I hate the Princess. Hang on, though: when
                Cuthbert kicks the bucket, she'll get to be Queen and then I'd
                be King.

                Number: Life is a Bowl of Cherries (CEDRIC)

CEDRIC   NO MORE HANGING AROUND —
                I'VE GOT MY FEET FIRMLY ON THE GROUND.
                WITH MY HEAD IN THE CLOUDS,
                I'M FEELING PROUD.
                LIFE IS A BOWL OF CHERRIES.

                JUST LIKE A SHOOTING STAR —
                I'M GONNA GO AMAZINGLY FAR.
                AND WHEN I GET TO THE TOP,
                I WON'T STOP.
                YES, LIFE IS A BOWL OF —

                (*Flash. Enter* CARABOSSE.)

                Crikey! Who are you?

CARABOSSE   Cedric?

CEDRIC   What's your game?

CARABOSSE   Sorry to frighten you: Carabosse the name.
                I need your help.

CEDRIC   How?

CARABOSSE   To steal the King's sword.

CEDRIC   What's in it for me?

CARABOSSE   A massive reward!

CEDRIC   Sorry. No go. I'm going to be King
              Myself soon. Won't be needing more money.
              See ya!

CARABOSSE   Don't you get smart with me, sonny.
              Unless you get that magic sword for me,
              I shall devise such tortures, I guarantee.
              Thumbscrews, the rack, stale school dinners, the third degree.
              You won't live to tell the tale. Which is it to be?

CEDRIC   Alright. Don't get you knickers in a twist:
              I'll do it —

CARABOSSE   Or you die!

CEDRIC   I get the gist.

CARABOSSE   Succeed, I'll let you live.

CEDRIC   Thanks very much.

CARABOSSE   You won't regret this.

CEDRIC   Fine —

CARABOSSE   I'll be in touch.

              (*Exit* CEDRIC *and* CARABOSSE. *Frontcloth out.*)

                            Scene Five

NANNY'S *kitchen.*

*Ancient equipment: old cooking range, dresser, sink with pots and pans to
ceiling: ie, months of washing up. Jars, bottles, etc. Crammed with every
conceivable ingredient. Large rectangular table, centre. There need be no
practical doors: entrances DR and DL.* NANNY *discovered putting
finishing touches to a pie.*

NANNY   Hello, dears!

AUDIENCE   Hello, Nanny Fanny Annie!

NANNY   (*louder*) Hello, dears!

AUDIENCE   Hello, Nanny Fanny Annie!

NANNY   And welcome to my kitchen! I've just finished cooking the King and Queen's supper: fig and rhubarb pie. That should keep them going for a bit. Seriously, though — the problem with being a cook is you put on so much weight. I got so fat I had to get my knickers on prescription. I went down to Bournemouth beach and they asked me to move so the tide could come in. I've been on a seafood diet. That hasn't worked either. Whenever I see food I eat it. When I was a girl I had an hourglass figure. What a waist! I could have had any man I pleased. Trouble was, I didn't please any of them. What a waste! Except my husband Ernie, of course. He was very taken by me. Well, grabbed really. He was a lovely man. He was a redhead. No hair — just a red head. Then one night I was sitting up in bed mending a puncture: he put his head round the door and said he was popping out to Tesco's for a tin of tuna, and he never came back. He never came back! He couldn't have got lost because he had a photographic memory. Pity he never got it developed. Or am I being a bit negative . . . ?

         (*Enter* HARRY *and* NUTS.)

HARRY   Hi, Ma!

NANNY   Hello, dears!

         (NUTS *starts jumping up and down, drawing attention to himself. Perhaps a cartwheel.*)

NANNY   What's up with Nuts?

HARRY   Hungry, I reckon, Ma.

NANNY   Time for a treat, Nuts?

         (*Renewed excitement from* NUTS.)

NANNY   I've saved three nutty buns for your tea.

         (*She throws them to* NUTS, *who catches them and juggles.*)

NANNY   Now, dears. Would you like to help ice the Princess's birthday cake? (*Great excitement from* NUTS *who puts on chef's hat.*)

HARRY   Yes please, Ma. Just tell us what to do.

NANNY   Right. Fetch me my recipe book . . .

HARRY   (*fetching book*) Fetch you your recipe book . . .

NANNY   And do exactly as I say!

HARRY   And do exactly as you say. Right.

             (NANNY *reads from the book. She is one end of the table so she can easily come down to the audience.* HARRY *is in the middle,* NUTS *as 'runner'.*)

NANNY   First take the cake.

HARRY   (*to* NUTS) First take the cake.

             (NUTS *takes the cake from the side and exits.*)

NANNY   (*re-capping*) First take the cake. Where's the cake?

HARRY   You told Nuts to take it.

NANNY   Not take the cake. 'Take the cake'. Nuts!

             (*Re-enter* NUTS *with the cake.*)

             Bring it here, Nuts. If you don't behave, I won't allow you to help.

             (NUTS *is crestfallen.*)

NANNY   Right — take the cake.

             (NUTS *perks up and goes to take it again then stops knowingly.*)

HARRY   The cake's a bit soft, Ma. (*The cake is a large square of foam/sponge.*) I don't reckon it's cooked.

NANNY   (*reading*) To test whether properly cooked — prick bottom with sharp fork.

HARRY   (*to* NUTS) Prick bottom with sharp fork.

             (NUTS *runs round to* NANNY'S *end of the table with long-pronged fork.*)

NANNY   (*re-capping*) Prick bottom with sharp fork. (NUTS *pricks her bottom.*) Aaarrhh! Not *my* bottom, you naughty monkey!

(Large spider descends over cake. Neither HARRY *nor* NUTS *sees it. Just as* NANNY *catches sight of it, it flies out.)*

(jumping) Ahh! *(To audience.)* What was that?

AUDIENCE	A spider!
NANNY	What?
AUDIENCE	A spider!
NANNY	A spider?
AUDIENCE	Yes!

NANNY   I'm having no spiders in my kitchen. I tell you what: if you see it again, will you shout out 'spider' as loudly as you can?

AUDIENCE	Yes!
NANNY	*Will* you?
AUDIENCE	YES!!

NANNY   Thank you, dears. Right — what next? *(Reading.)* One bag of icing sugar.

HARRY   *(to* NUTS*)* One bag of icing sugar.

*(*NUTS *gets bag of icing sugar.)*

NANNY   *(re-capping)* One bag of icing sugar.

(A second spider comes down in a different place: behind NANNY *this time.)*

AUDIENCE   Spider!

NANNY   Where?

*(*NUTS *and* HARRY *see it too.)*

AUDIENCE   Behind you! *(Etc.)*
HARRY

NANNY   Behind me? Where? *(Etc.)*

(When she eventually looks behind, the spider has gone.)

NANNY ⟩ You're pulling my leg. There was no spider.

AUDIENCE   There was!
HARRY

NANNY   Oh no there wasn't!

AUDIENCE   Oh yes there was! (*Etc x 3.*)
HARRY

NANNY ⟩ Oh, alright then — I believe you. But you'll have to tell me
       much quicker next time.

HARRY   What next, Ma?

NANNY ⟩ Take one large bowl —

HARRY   What, Ma?

NANNY   Bowl.

HARRY   (*to* NUTS) Bowl! (NUTS *looks puzzled.*)

NANNY   (*loudly and slowly*) Bowl!
HARRY

             (NUTS *take a very soft ball and makes to bowl: long run up
             across the stage.*)

VOICE   And it's Nuts coming into bowl — right arm over the wicket,
OVER ⟩ and . . .

             (HARRY, *using, say, a very large flat cheese grater, hits the
             ball for six over the audience.*)

VOICE   . . . it's six runs!
OVER

             (*Recorded polite applause.*)

NANNY   Not 'bowl' you daft primate — bowl! Doh!

             (NANNY *gets the mixing bowl herself.*)

HARRY   Sorry, Ma!

NANNY   If you want a thing doing, do it yourself.

HARRY   What next, Ma?

NANNY   (*reading*) Empty icing sugar into bowl.

HARRY   (*to* NUTS) Empty icing sugar into bowl.

NANNY   (*re-capping*) Empty icing sugar into bowl.

               (NUTS *does so: clouds of white powder.*)

NANNY   And add a little flour.

HARRY   (*to* NUTS) And add a little flower.

               (NUTS *produces huge sunflower.*)

NANNY   (*to* NUTS) A *little* flower.
HARRY

               (NUTS *holds up a small drooping flower.*)

HARRY   What sort of little flower, Ma?

NANNY   }   Self-raising.

HARRY   (*to* NUTS) Self-raising flower.

               (*The small flower straightens up and* NUTS *puts it into the
               bowl.*)

NANNY   (*reading*) And stir in one pint of cold water.

HARRY   (*to* NUTS) Stir in one pint of cold water.

               (*As* HARRY *and* NUTS *start to do this, a third spider appears.*)

AUDIENCE   Spider!

               (NANNY *at first pretends not to hear. When she does, she
               swishes at it — Tarzan-style, with broom — and it flies out.*)

NANNY   Thank you, dears!

HARRY   Ready, Ma! We've made the icing.

NANNY   Final ingredient: (*Reading.*) for that unusual flavouring —
               add a little thyme.

HARRY   What's thyme, Ma?

NANNY   About half past five.

               (*Enter* BRIAR ROSE.)

BRIAR ROSE Hi, Nanny!

NANNY   Hello, your loyal Princessness. I'm not sure you should be
               down here, dear. The King and Queen don't like it.

BRIAR ROSE I don't care. There's nothing to do upstairs. Hi, Harry!

HARRY   Hello, Princess. You're just in time to help ice your cake.

BRIAR ROSE Where's the icing?

HARRY   Nuts — let me have the icing.

               (NUTS *looks puzzled.*)

               The icing. (*More deliberately.*) The icing: let me have it!

               (NUTS *takes great glob of icing and lands it on* HARRY'S *head.*)

HARRY   Nuts!

NANNY   You naughty monkey!

HARRY   I'll get you!

               (HARRY *scoops up some icing onto plate. Brief chase round
               table.*)

NANNY   Behave yourselves, both of you. Princess, don't encourage
               them. Harry! (*Etc.*)

               (*Enter* L C.)

L C   Come along, Cedric.

               (L C *gets* HARRY'S *plate of icing full in the face.*)

BRIAR ROSE Run, Harry! Quick! Nuts, hide!

               (*Exit* HARRY. NUTS *hides behind table. The chef's hat is
               visible over the top. Enter* CEDRIC.)

L C   Who is responsible for this outrage?

NANNY   Well you see, Elsie . . .

L C   And *don't* call me Elsie!

NANNY   Sorry, Els . . . Else . . . what else shall I call you, Else?

CEDRIC   I bet it was Harry, father. And that nasty monkey.

BRIAR ROSE   Don't tell tales, Cedric.

L C   The King and Queen have some very important news for you,
               Princess.

BRIAR ROSE   What sort of news?

QUEEN   (*off*) Elsie!

CEDRIC   You'll see.

               (*Enter* QUEEN, *followed by* KING.)

QUEEN   Come along, Cuthbert — don't dawdle. Elsie — what's that
               mess on your face? Briar Rose — I thought I told you to stay
               upstairs. Nanny — this kitchen is a disgrace. I can smell that
               monkey! Monkey — come out!

CEDRIC   (*seeing chef's hat moving along back of table*) There it is!

L C   Come out! Come out, you horrible animal!

               (NUTS *emerges.*)

QUEEN   Why's it got that silly hat on?

NANNY   He's been doing the icing, your massiveness.

KING   Fondant icing?

NANNY   Of course I'm fond of icing or I wouldn't be doing it!

QUEEN   The standards of hygiene in this culinary establishment are
               quite deplorable. Cuthbert — *do* something!

L C   In view of Cedric's promotion to Royal Consort, your
               majesticality, may I suggest he is made Keeper of the Royal
               Monkey.

CEDRIC   Then I can lock the nasty creature up!

BRIAR ROSE   No!

QUEEN   Brilliant!

L C   In a cage!

BRIAR ROSE   You can't!

QUEEN   Capital!

BRIAR ROSE   Father?

KING   Well, my dear, your mother does seem to think . . .

BRIAR ROSE   And what did he mean, "Cedric's promotion to Royal
              Consort"?

L C   That's the important news.

QUEEN   Owing to the lamentable shortage of Princes in the vicinity,
              we have decided that you must marry Cedric.

BRIAR ROSE   No!

KING   I'm sure he'll make a most adequate husband, my dear.

BRIAR ROSE   I won't!

NANNY   Well said, dear.

QUEEN   Nanny, be quiet!

CEDRIC   Dearest!

BRIAR ROSE   Ugh! Go away! I won't marry you. I won't, I won't, I won't!

CEDRIC   Temper, temper.

QUEEN   Give her time. Come along, Cuthbert.

              (*Exit* QUEEN.)

BRIAR ROSE   Father?

QUEEN   (*off*) Cuthbert!

KING   (*to* BRIAR ROSE) I'm sorry, my dear.

            (*Exit* KING.)

L C   Try to be nice to the Princess, Cedric.

NANNY   Fat chance!

L C   Nanny!

NANNY   Yes, dear?

L C   The two lovebirds want to be left alone.

BRIAR ROSE   They don't!

L C   Forget Briar Rose. Think of me for a change.

NANNY   I think of little else.

L C   And *don't* call me Little Else.

            (*He drags* NANNY *off.*)

CEDRIC   Briar Rose —

BRIAR ROSE   Go away!

CEDRIC   (*particularly odious*) I think you're really pretty.

BRIAR ROSE   (*backing off*) Cedric —

CEDRIC   Can I kiss you?

BRIAR ROSE   No, you can't.

CEDRIC   But we're going to be married.

BRIAR ROSE   I wouldn't marry you in a million years.

CEDRIC   Please.

BRIAR ROSE   No! Cedric! No!

            (NUTS *leaps off table and fights* CEDRIC. *Heroic music. "Superman".*)

CEDRIC   I'll get you, you vicious beast.

            (CEDRIC *makes to go.*)

BRIAR ROSE Cedric.

CEDRIC   What?

BRIAR ROSE Would you like to lick the bowl before you go?

CEDRIC   Yeah! Hang on — is this a trick?

BRIAR ROSE No!

CEDRIC   Are you sure?

BRIAR ROSE Yes!

CEDRIC   (*to audience*) Shall I lick the bowl?

AUDIENCE   Yes!

CEDRIC   Shall I?

AUDIENCE   YES!!

CEDRIC   Alright, then.

            (NUTS *holds bowl so even* CEDRIC *is finally aware it's going over his head.*)

CEDRIC   (*at last moment*) It *is* a trick. I've changed my mind.

            (*He makes to go. All three spiders come down.*)

AUDIENCE   Spider!

            (CEDRIC *looks up and freezes.* NUTS *upturns bowl on* CEDRIC's *head. Spiders fly out.* NUTS *replaces bowl.*)

CEDRIC   I'll . . . I'll . . .

BRIAR ROSE Temper, temper, Cedric!

CEDRIC   I'll . . . !

            (CEDRIC *exits, wailing.*)

BRIAR ROSE   Thanks, Nuts! You were brilliant!

(*Enter* HARRY, *laughing*.)

HARRY   What's up with Cedric?

BRIAR ROSE   Things are serious, Harry.

HARRY   What?

BRIAR ROSE   Nuts is going to be locked up in a cage. And I've got to marry Cedric! All on account of a shortage of Princes.

HARRY   That's wicked!

BRIAR ROSE   I've refused, of course.

HARRY   I wish I were a Prince. I'd take you away from all this.

BRIAR ROSE   We could escape — you and me and Nuts.

HARRY   Where to?

BRIAR ROSE   Anywhere. Listen: if we tried to go today we'd get caught. So. I'll *pretend* to agree to marry Cedric. I'll say I've changed my mind and like him after all.

HARRY   That'll put everybody off guard.

BRIAR ROSE   Exactly. Then we'll slip away in three days' time. On my birthday. Just before the wedding.

NANNY   (*off*) Harry!

HARRY   Sh! Here comes Ma.

(*Enter* NANNY.)

NANNY   Harry — there you are, dear. Have you heard the news?

BRIAR ROSE   I've been thinking, Nanny. Cedric's not so bad after all.

NANNY   Eh?

BRIAR ROSE   He is the Lord Chancellor's son.

NANNY   That's true and Elsie's a fine man.

BRIAR ROSE So I've decided to marry him.

NANNY Who — Elsie?

BRIAR ROSE No! Cedric.

HARRY Isn't that wonderful, Ma?

NANNY Well, I suppose if you're both happy — I'm happy. Oooh! I do love a good wedding.

QUEEN (*entering*) Come along, Cuthbert!

(KING, L C *and* CEDRIC *follow*.)

KING Come along, Elsie!

L C Come along, Cedric!

QUEEN Now then, daughter. I trust you've come to your senses.

BRIAR ROSE Yes, Mama. I agree to marry Cedric.

QUEEN Then you are a naughty, ungrateful, disobedient — eh?

KING What?

L C Well!

CEDRIC Cripes!

BRIAR ROSE My Ceddy-weddy! (*She kisses him.*)

CEDRIC (*aside*) Yuk! (*To* BRIAR ROSE.) My Briar Rosy-posy! (*He kisses her.*)

BRIAR ROSE (*aside*) Yuk! (*To* QUEEN.) On my birthday, I think you said, Mama!

KING A double celebration!

QUEEN I'm deliriously happy!

Number: The Happiest Day of my Life!
(*Full Company — except* TIME FAIRY *and* CARABOSSE)

QUEEN (*to* KING) IT'S JUST WHAT I WANTED, IT'S JUST HOW I
PLANNED,

A SUITABLE SUITOR FOR BRIAR ROSE' HAND.
I'VE WATCHED AND I'VE WAITED, I'VE PLOTTED
AND SCHEMED,

KING   NOW MY DAUGHTER WILL MARRY THE MAN OF —

QUEEN   — *MY* DREAMS.

BOTH   NO MORE TROUBLE AND STRIFE,
FOR THIS IS THE HAPPIEST DAY OF MY LIFE!

ALL   NO MORE TROUBLE AND STRIFE,
FOR THIS IS THE HAPPIEST DAY OF MY LIFE!

L C   *(to* CEDRIC) I'M SO VERY DELIGHTED, WE'VE DONE IT,
MY BOY!
MY CEDRIC A PRINCE! WHAT A TRIUMPH! WHAT JOY!

CEDRIC   NO MORE WILL THE COURTIERS ALL LAUGH IN MY FACE.
AS THE FUTURE KING, I'LL PUT THEM ALL IN THEIR
PLACE.

BOTH   NO MORE TROUBLE AND STRIFE,
FOR THIS IS THE HAPPIEST DAY OF MY LIFE!

ALL   NO MORE TROUBLE AND STRIFE,
FOR THIS IS THE HAPPIEST DAY OF MY LIFE!

BRIAR ROSE   *(to* HARRY) I'M EVER SO PLEASED THAT WE'VE THOUGHT
OF A PLAN.
DO YOU THINK WE CAN DO IT?

HARRY   I KNOW THAT WE CAN!
BUT WE'VE GOT TO BE QUIET.

BRIAR ROSE   WE'VE GOT TO BE QUICK.
IF I HAVE TO WED CEDRIC, I THINK I'LL BE SICK!

BOTH   NO MORE TROUBLE AND STRIFE,
FOR THIS IS THE HAPPIEST DAY OF MY LIFE!

ALL   NO MORE TROUBLE AND STRIFE,
FOR THIS IS THE HAPPIEST DAY OF MY LIFE!

NANNY   WHO WOULD HAVE THOUGHT IT? MY BABY A BRIDE!
I'M STARTING TO FEEL A BIT FUNNY INSIDE.
I'M SNIFFLING AND SNUFFLING, I'VE NO IDEA WHY.
I'M HAPPY AS LARRY, BUT I'M GOING TO CRY —

BOO! HOO! (*Etc, as Chorus.*)

ALL   BOO! HOO! (*Etc, as Chorus.*)

(*Flash. Enter* CARABOSSE. *Company freeze.*)

CARABOSSE   Perfection! It's almost going *too* well!
They think they're happy: Time alone will tell.
My stratagems all gather to a head —
In three days' time the Princess will be dead!
It's all too easy — makes me laugh.
I'll see *you* in the second half!

(*Exit* CARABOSSE. *Number resumes.*)

ALL   SO ROLL OUT THE CARPET, AND STRIKE UP THE BAND:
SPREAD THE GLAD TIDINGS THROUGHOUT ALL THE LAND.

KING   MAY ALL OF MY SUBJECTS BE MERRY AND GAY,

QUEEN   MAKE READY FOR BRIAR ROSE' WEDDING DAY.

(CHILDREN *join.*)

ALL   NO MORE TROUBLE AND STRIFE,
FOR THIS IS THE HAPPIEST DAY OF MY LIFE!
NO MORE TROUBLE AND STRIFE —
FOR THIS IS THE HAPPIEST
DAY OF MY LIFE!

(*Frontcloth in. Interval.*)

ACT TWO

Scene One

Frontcloth.

Flash. Enter CARABOSSE.

CARABOSSE   It's me again! Lovely to see you all:
I trust you had a horrid Interval.
Too much chocolate? Yuk! You greedy lot.
I hope your tummies ache, and your teeth rot!
Don't think you've come to have a good time:
I'm here to wreck your wretched pantomime.
Hiss! Boo! Yes, I love it! Back to the plot:
The princess dies today — like it or not.
I need that magic sword . . .

(*Enter* CEDRIC.)

CEDRIC   It's her! Oh, dear!

CARABOSSE   Then I'll have the power. Cedric, come 'ere!
Got the magic sword?

CEDRIC   Sorry — I forgot.
What with the wedding and all . . .

CARABOSSE   You great clot!
You promised to steal it — I'd make you rich.

CEDRIC   Well you see, I'm afraid there's a slight hitch —

CARABOSSE   Yes?

CEDRIC   Stealing's a crime. I'd lose my head
If I got caught.

CARABOSSE   Then either way — you're dead!
Don't get caught, fool! Be rich! But if you fail,
Sunshine —

CEDRIC   What?

CARABOSSE   You won't live to tell the tale.

CEDRIC   OK. So, what do I have to do?

CARABOSSE   Right.
            First catch that wretched monkey —

CEDRIC   It might bite!

CARABOSSE   Don't tell me you're frightened!

CEDRIC   No!

CARABOSSE   Then act your age!

CEDRIC   OK. Then what?

CARABOSSE   Lock it up.

CEDRIC   (*with relish*) In a tiny cage!

CARABOSSE   That's more like it. Then —

CEDRIC   (*keen*) Yes?

CARABOSSE   Tell the princess
            That you'll kill her precious monkey — *unless*
            She gets you the sword.

CEDRIC   How —

CARABOSSE   She'll ask the king:
            He'll do anything for her — anything.
            That's no problem. Then she'll give the sword to you.
            To save that nasty monkey that's the least she'll do.

CEDRIC   Er . . .

CARABOSSE   No ifs, no buts. Then you hand it over:
            I'm happy! You're rich! We're both in clover!
            (*Sings.*) "Who wants to be a millionaire?"

CEDRIC   (*sings*) "I do!"

CARABOSSE   Off you go then.

CEDRIC   Right!

            (*Exit* CEDRIC.)

CARABOSSE   He hasn't got a clue!

I'll betray him, of course — well, wouldn't you?
Soon the sword will be mine: absolute power!
And Briar Rose will die within the hour!

(*Exit* CARABOSSE. *Frontcloth out.*)

Scene Two

The Royal Hall.

Some extra decoration for birthday and planned wedding.

KING *marches on, wearing his magic sword and some armour. He is*
followed by rabble of CHILDREN, *with their own military gear and toy*
swords. NUTS *is also in the squad.*

KING   Left right. Left right. Left right. Squad . . . halt!

               (CHILDREN *bump into each other and fall over.*)

               Come on, you rabble! Don't you know how to march? Look
               I'll show you.

               (*He demonstrates marching as he begins the song.*)

               Number: A Soldier's Life (KING *and* CHILDREN)

KING   A SOLDIER'S LIFE IS THE LIFE FOR ME:
               IT'S WHAT I'VE ALWAYS LONGED TO BE.
               MARCHING UP AND DOWN WITH MY HEAD HELD HIGH:
               YOU CAN DO IT TOO IF YOU REALLY TRY.

               (*He inspects his troops.*)

               FIRST YOU'VE GOT TO STAND UP STRAIGHT AND TALL,
               DON'T MOVE A MUSCLE TILL I GIVE THE CALL —
               WHEN YOU'RE READY — I WILL SHOUT,
               AND THAT'S YOUR CUE TO MARCH ABOUT . . .

               (*spoken*) Ready? Squad! By the left! March!

               LEFT RIGHT, LEFT RIGHT,
               MARCHING UP AND DOWN,
               MARCHING THROUGH THE COUNTRY,
               MARCHING THROUGH . . .

(He breaks off because the CHILDREN *have marched off in the wrong direction, led by* NUTS, *who is generally playing up.)*

KING   *(spoken)* Halt! Come back! *(They return.)* Alright. Follow me. Very slowly. Here we go . . .

(sung) LEFT RIGHT, LEFT RIGHT,
MARCHING UP AND DOWN.
MARCHING THROUGH THE COUNTRY,
MARCHING THROUGH THE TOWN.
IT'S SO MUCH FUN, IT'S ABSOLUTELY GRAND
TO BE MARCHING WITH THE FINEST ARMY IN THE LAND!

(After a tentative start they march well, and execute an increasingly impressive formation march during an instrumental section. Then, still marching:)

ALL   LEFT RIGHT, LEFT RIGHT,
MARCHING UP AND DOWN.
MARCHING THROUGH THE COUNTRY,
MARCHING THROUGH THE TOWN.
IT'S SO MUCH FUN, IT'S ABSOLUTELY GRAND
TO BE MARCHING WITH THE FINEST ARMY IN THE LAND.
IT'S SO MUCH FUN, IT'S ABSOLUTELY GRAND,
AND NOW WE ARE THE FINEST ARMY IN THE LAND!

(Enter QUEEN.*)*

QUEEN   Cuthbert! Go away, you messy children! And you, monkey — shoo, shoo, shoo!

(Exit NUTS *and* CHILDREN.*)*

I'm in a very good mood today, Cuthbert.

KING   Me too. I've been polishing my magic sword —

QUEEN   Magic! Huh! It's Briar Rose's sixteenth birthday.

KING   I know. I'm jolly excited!

QUEEN   And she's getting married.

KING   *(dubious)* To Cedric.

QUEEN   To Cedric.

(Enter CEDRIC *in absurd wedding gear.)*

CEDRIC   To me!

QUEEN   Oh, Cedric! You do look nice!

CEDRIC   And may I say, your queenliness, how perfectly picturesque you are looking too.

QUEEN   How kind.

              (*Sound of Time-o-bile arriving.*)

QUEEN   Cuthbert, what's that noise?

KING   Probably just an invasion, my dear.

              (*The Time-o-bile begins to descend. Flashing lights as before. Smoke for landing.*)

KING   (*realisation*) Invasion! Help! (*He dashes around, brandishing his sword.*) Elsie! Help!

              (*Enter L C.*)

L C   With respect, your majesticality — it's only the Time Fairy. She attended the christening — remember?

QUEEN   I remember her well. She got it all wrong. Something about putting Briar Rose to sleep for a hundred years.

L C   Ridiculous!

KING   Nonsensical!

QUEEN   Absurd!

              (*Flash. The* TIME FAIRY *steps out of the Time-o-bile.*)

TIME FAIRY   Not as daft as you think. Upon my word —
              Have you forgotten Carabosse's curse?
              I did my best — it could have been worse.
              Just fancy! Briar Rose — sixteen today!
              Doesn't Time fly! Where is she, anyway?

L C   No idea.

TIME FAIRY   What!!

L C   Calm down.

KING   After the christening —

TIME FAIRY   Listen, please —

QUEEN   We destroyed —

TIME FAIRY   Listen!

QUEEN   We are listening.

KING   Every spinning wheel for miles around.

L C   We also kept the princess palace-bound.

QUEEN   Closely guarded when she played outside.

KING   She couldn't prick her finger if she tried.

TIME FAIRY   Then why was Carabosse here three days ago?

QUEEN   Cuthbert?

KING   Elsie?

TIME FAIRY   You mean, you didn't know?

QUEEN   Find Briar Rose! Quick! Before it's too late!
             Cuthbert!

             (*Exit* QUEEN.)

KING   Alright, dear. Don't get in a state!

             (*Exit* KING.)

TIME FAIRY   We'll look this way. Elsie!

L C   Dear, oh dear!

TIME FAIRY   Come on!

L C   What a fuss!

TIME FAIRY   Cedric — you stay here.

             (*Exit* L C *and* TIME FAIRY.)

CEDRIC Great! Now to catch the monkey like what Carabosse said I had to. I've got three of his favourite nutty buns as bait. (*He lays the buns as a trail.*) One — two —three. When he gets to the last one, I'll lower the cage — like this — just you watch — very slowly . . . (*He demonstrates by lowering the cage with a pulley. It should have no door.*) . . . and I've got him! (*Cage up again.*) Easy peasie, lemon squeezie! (*To audience.*) You won't warn Nuts, will you?

AUDIENCE Yes!

CEDRIC Oh no you won't!

AUDIENCE Oh yes we will! (*Etc.*)

CEDRIC Oh . . . well, he'll be too busy eating to take any notice of you. (*Calls.*) Nuts! Nuts! Nuts! Shh! Here he comes . . .

(*Enter* NUTS. CEDRIC *hides by the pulley.* NUTS *finds the first and second buns, rubbing tummy with expectation. As he goes for the third the audience will be screaming. Just as the cage is about to reach* NUTS, *he comes down to see what all the fuss is about and the cage misses him. Flash. Exit* NUTS. *Enter* CARABOSSE.)

Carabosse You dozy dingbat!

CEDRIC I was a bit slow . . .

CARABOSSE You dope! You dunce!

CEDRIC I'll have another go.

CARABOSSE See this white powder?

CEDRIC Sugar.

CARABOSSE Don't be daft! Take it.

CEDRIC What is it, then?

CARABOSSE A sleeping draught.
Sprinkle it on a bun, just like icing.
Nuts will love it — most enticing.
It'll only take the smallest bite —
One taste —

CEDRIC   And he'll go out like a light!

CARABOSSE   Exactly! So, next time he'll be off-guard
             When you lower the cage. I've marked your card,
             Cedric: so far I'm not your greatest fan.
             Fail me this time, and you're a dead man!

             (*Exit* CARABOSSE.)

CEDRIC   Oooh, she does give me the willies!

             (*Enter* HARRY.)

HARRY   Cedric — (CEDRIC *jumps*.) Seen Briar Rose?

CEDRIC   No and I wouldn't tell you if I had!

             (*Exit* CEDRIC.)

HARRY   Who's rattled his cage?

             (*Enter* BRIAR ROSE, *not dressed for wedding*.)

BRIAR ROSE Is the coast clear?

HARRY   Briar Rose! Are you ready to go?

BRIAR ROSE You bet! I've got to marry Cedric in half an hour. But where's
             Nuts?

HARRY   I thought he was with you.

BRIAR ROSE Oh no!

HARRY   (*calling*) Nuts!

BRIAR ROSE (*louder*) Nuts!

BOTH   (*very loud*) Nuts! (*To each other*.) Shh! (*Quietly*.) Nuts!

BRIAR ROSE We can't go without him.

HARRY   I'll look in the kitchen.

BRIAR ROSE And I'll search the garden.

HARRY   See you back here in five minutes.

BRIAR ROSE   Right.

(*Exit* HARRY. *Enter* TIME FAIRY. BRIAR ROSE *almost bumps into her as she goes.*)

BRIAR ROSE   Oops! Sorry! Who are you?

TIME FAIRY   The Time Fairy.

BRIAR ROSE   Who?

TIME FAIRY   I'm your Godmother. Hi!

BRIAR ROSE   I'm wary
Of strangers.

TIME FAIRY   How wise — especially today.

BRIAR ROSE   Why? What do you mean?

TIME FAIRY   I'd rather not say.

BRIAR ROSE   Explain — please . . .

TIME FAIRY   I've no wish to alarm you.
Stick with me and nobody will harm you.

BRIAR ROSE   (*aside*) I think she's a bit dotty, the poor dear.
Where are you from?

TIME FAIRY   Time. I hop from year to year.

BRIAR ROSE   (*aside*) I'll humour her. (*To* TIME FAIRY.) What's that?

TIME FAIRY   My Time-o-bile.
Want to know how it works? It's no big deal.
On the first dial is the length of your flight —
D for Days, M for Months, Y for Years — right?
This one is marked one to a hundred, by degree.
So — if I set it say, to sixty-three,
The first dial to D, and this arrow to B —
I'd fly backward in Time sixty-three days.

BRIAR ROSE   (*drawn in now*) I see!
Let me get this right: F means 'forward' and B 'back' —

TIME FAIRY   Exactly! You're smart! I reckon you've got the knack.

BRIAR ROSE How does it start?

TIME FAIRY   Ah — to begin the ride
            Somebody has to be sitting inside
            With the door shut. You don't believe a word, do you?

BRIAR ROSE I didn't at first, but now — yes — I think I do.

TIME FAIRY Are you OK? You're looking a bit queer.

BRIAR ROSE No no — I'm fine. (*Aside.*) I've had an idea! (*To* TIME FAIRY.)
            Excuse me. Change of plan. I have to fly.
            Must find Harry — and Nuts — and, er . . . goodbye!

            (*Exit* BRIAR ROSE.)

TIME FAIRY Odd girl! But then, look at her mum and dad:
            Bonkers, both of them: quite, quite mad!
            I ask you: who'd be a godmother?

NANNY   (*off*) Nuts!

TIME FAIRY Talking of nutcases — here comes another!

            (*Exit* TIME FAIRY. *Enter* NANNY, *with three buns.*)

NANNY   Hello, dears!

AUDIENCE   Hello, Nanny Fanny Annie!

NANNY   Nuts! Nutty bun time! Where are you?

            (*Enter* L C.)

L C   (*putting his arm round her waist*) Nanny!

NANNY   Ooh, Elsie! Don't! Stop! (*He takes his arm away. She puts
            them back.*) Don't stop!

L C   Nanny! My favourite nutty buns. You shouldn't have.

NANNY   They're not for you . . .

L C   I hope you're not still feeding that monkey.

NANNY   Nuts? No . . . I was just checking I'd remembered everything for the party. Nuts — dates — yoghurts. Ah! I've forgotten the yoghurts.

L C   Then order some.

NANNY   Who from?

L C   The milkman, who else? (*He goes to the Time-o-bile.*) Look — a milk machine.

NANNY   But that's not a —

L C   Nanny. Who's the Lord Chancellor?

NANNY   You are, but —

L C   Thank you. Look. M for Milk. Got enough milk?

NANNY   Yes, but it's not a —

L C   Nanny. Don't try to teach your grandmother to pluck legs.

NANNY   It's 'suck eggs'.

L C   What?

NANNY   Eggs.

L C   Eggs? Oh, that's D for Dairy.

NANNY   I give up!

L C   And Y for Yoghurt. Got enough yoghurts?

NANNY   Well, Harry likes yogs, and —

L C   Say 100?

NANNY   It is a big do.

L C   Then 100 it is. This arrow says F or B.

NANNY   F or B . . .

L C   Fresh or Bad!

NANNY   He's flaming mad!

L C   You don't want 100 bad yoghurts. I'll set it to fresh. (*He sets the three dials*.) There we are . . .

NANNY   Ain't he wonderful with his hands!

L C   . . . 100 Fresh Yoghurts. (*He bangs the machine*.) Wouldn't you know it! It's empty. I'll go and give the milkman a rocket. He's bound to be floating around somewhere. Milko! Milko!

        (*Exit* L C.)

NANNY   Nutty as a suitcase! But isn't he gorgeous! (*Remembering*.) Nuts!

        (*Enter* CEDRIC.)

CEDRIC   Nanny, I bet you're really busy today. I'll find Nuts if you like and give him his tea.

NANNY   Thank you, dear. (*She gives him three buns*.) There you are: three nutty buns. (*To audience*.) And to think I never used to like him.

        (*Exit* NANNY.)

CEDRIC   Now — (*He lays out the buns as before*.) One. Two. And sleeping powder on the biggest and nuttiest. (*He sprinkles it on*.) Three. Nuts! Nuts! Nuts! Shh! Here he comes again.

        (*He hides by the pulley ready to lower cage. Enter* NUTS. *He takes the first two buns. Under the cage he bites into the third. Instant attack of sleep. Slump. Cage in*.)

CEDRIC   (*triumphant*) Ha-ha! Now I've caught the monkey, I can have anything I like!

        Number: Life is a Bowl of Cherries (CEDRIC)

CEDRIC   ALL MY LIFE I'VE WANTED TO BE NUMBER ONE —
TO CALL THE SHOTS, TO MAKE IT, TO HAVE LOTS OF FUN.
BUT UP TO NOW I'VE ALWAYS PLAYED SECOND FIDDLE.
BETWEEN THE PRINCESS AND HARRY, I WAS STUCK
                         IN THE MIDDLE.
BUT NOW AT LAST MY OPPORTUNITY'S HERE:
A FUTURE LIFE BECKONS: IT ALL SEEMS TO BE
                         CRYSTAL CLEAR.

NO MORE HANGING AROUND —
I'VE GOT MY FEET FIRMLY ON THE GROUND.
WITH MY HEAD IN THE CLOUDS,
I'M FEELING PROUD.
LIFE IS A BOWL OF CHERRIES.

JUST LIKE A SHOOTING STAR —
I'M GONNA GO AMAZINGLY FAR.
AND WHEN I GET TO THE TOP,
I WON'T STOP.
YES, LIFE IS A BOWL OF CHERRIES.

AND OH, THAT MAGICAL FEELING —
JUST TO KNOW, AT LAST YOU ARE THERE.
THE OH, SO POWERFUL FEELING,
THAT EVERYONE WILL BOW AND SCRAPE,
WHEN I'VE GOT THEM IN MY CLUTCHES
THERE'LL BE NO ESCAPE.

I'M SINGING IN THE RAIN,
IN THE RAIN I WILL SING.
WHAT A GLORIOUS FEELING:
I'M GONNA TO BE KING.
TONIGHT, TONIGHT,
AT LAST I'VE GOT IT RIGHT.
AND FOR ONCE IN A LIFETIME,
I FEEL LIKE A GIANT.
AND I'M OVER THE RAINBOW,
WAY UP HIGH.
FOR WHEN I RULE THE WORLD,
ALL MY SUBJECTS WILL BE PAYING LOTS OF TAX.
THEY WILL WORK SO HARD
THAT IT WILL BREAK THEIR BACKS.
BUT I'LL HAVE
NO, NO REGRETS!
NO, I WILL HAVE NO REGRETS!
FOR I WILL BE KING CEDRIC,
TYRANT OF THE FREE.
NOW I'LL BE YOUR MONARCH —
NOT JUST THE SON OF L C.
AND I WILL CLIMB EVERY MOUNTAIN,
FORD EVERY STREAM.
EVEN MARRY THE PRINCESS,
THEN I'LL HAVE MY DREAM.

SO — CURTAIN UP, LIGHT THE LIGHTS —
ABSOLUTE POWER IS WITHIN MY SIGHTS.
IT'LL BE SO MUCH FUN

WHEN I'M NUMBER ONE:
LIFE IS A BOWL OF CHERRIES.

I'M GONNA HAVE A BALL:
BEING RULER OVER ALL.
I WILL DANCE AND SING
'COS I'M GONNA TO BE KING.
YES, LIFE IS A BOWL OF CHERRIES AND APRICOTS,
LIFE IS A BASIN OF ICE-CREAM AND COCOA-POPS.
LIFE IS A BUCKET OF PIZZA AND JELLY
AND SAUSAGES, BAKED BEANS, SPAGHETTI,
FISH FINGERS AND STEW!
AND I AM NOT GOING TO GIVE ANY TO YOU!
BUT I'LL COVER THE WHOLE LOT
WITH CHOCOLATE FUDGE TOPPING SO THICK:
AND MOUTHFUL BY MOUTHFUL
I'LL EAT IT UNTIL
I AM SICK!

CEDRIC   Now to get the magic sword!

BRIAR ROSE   (*off*) Nuts!

             (*Enter* BRIAR ROSE.)

BRIAR ROSE   Oh! Cedric — have you seen Nuts?

CEDRIC   Yes, but he can't see you!

BRIAR ROSE   What? (*She sees cage and screams.*) Nuts!

             (*Enter* HARRY.)

HARRY   What's going on?

BRIAR ROSE   It's Nuts!

HARRY   Is he dead?

BRIAR ROSE   No — he's still breathing.

             (NUTS *can begin to recover quite rapidly here.*)

CEDRIC   Not for much longer he won't be unless . . .

BRIAR ROSE   Unless what?

CEDRIC   . . . you get me your dad's magic sword.

BRIAR ROSE What do you want that for?

CEDRIC Ask no questions and you'll be told no lies:
But if I don't get that sword — the monkey dies!

(*Reaction from* NUTS.)

BRIAR ROSE Cedric!

CEDRIC I mean it.

(*Exit* CEDRIC.)

HARRY He's serious.

BRIAR ROSE What can we do? There's no way into the cage.

HARRY We'll just have to get the sword.

BRIAR ROSE How?

HARRY Easy. The king's wearing it today for the first time ever. I'll
find a way of taking it when he's not looking.

BRIAR ROSE What if he catches you?

HARRY I'll have my head chopped off!

BRIAR ROSE But —

HARRY Don't worry. I'll give the sword straight to Cedric and tell the
king that he's got it.

BRIAR ROSE Father will be furious!

HARRY Exactly — and in all the hullabaloo, it'll be dead easy for us
to escape with Nuts.

BRIAR ROSE Brilliant!

QUEEN (*off*) Cuthbert!

HARRY Sh! They're coming. Quick — hide!

(BRIAR ROSE *hides. Enter* QUEEN, KING, L C *and* CEDRIC.)

QUEEN Come along, Cuthbert!

KING   Yes, dear.

L C   I'm sure I heard the princess's voice.

CEDRIC   And I saw her.

QUEEN   Well, she's not here now, is she!

HARRY   Permission to speak, your highnesses.

QUEEN   What is it, you stupid boy?

HARRY   The princess *was* here.

            (*He comes to stand close to the* KING.)

KING   When?

HARRY   Just now.

QUEEN   Here?

HARRY   Here.

L C   Here.

KING   Hear, hear!

QUEEN   She's *not* here.

L C   But she *was* here.

CEDRIC   That's the point.

L C   That's the point.

KING   *What's* the point?

L C   (*giving up*) What's the point?

QUEEN   The point is, if she *was* here, she must be somewhere.

KING   That's what *I* said!

QUEEN   Come along, Cuthbert!

            (*Exit* QUEEN.)

KING   Yes, dear. Come along, Elsie!

(Exit KING. HARRY *slides the sword out of its scabbard as* KING *goes.)*

L C   Yes, dear. Come along, Cedric!

(Exit L C. CEDRIC *makes to go.)*

CEDRIC   Yes, dear.

HARRY   Cedric!

CEDRIC   Wot?

HARRY   The sword!

(BRIAR ROSE *comes out of hiding.)*

CEDRIC   *(aggressive)* Give it here!

BRIAR ROSE   Remember your promise, Cedric.

CEDRIC   Yeah, yeah.

BRIAR ROSE   To release Nuts.

CEDRIC   Give me the sword first. That was your part of the bargain.

HARRY   *(important decision)* Alright.

(HARRY *hands over the sword.* CEDRIC *snatches it, and threatens them.)*

CEDRIC   How stupid can you get? You can forget your rotten monkey!

KING   *(off)* I've lost my sword!

HARRY   You cheat!

KING   *(off)* Where's my magic sword?

CEDRIC   Harry!

HARRY   What?

CEDRIC   *(throwing sword)* Catch! (HARRY *catches.)*

KING   (*entering*) Who's stolen my sword?

HARRY   Oh, no!

                (*Enter* QUEEN, NANNY *and* L C.)

L C   Call the police!

CEDRIC   There's the thief! (*Chase may start here.*)

NANNY   Harry!

BRIAR ROSE   No!

KING   Seize him!

QUEEN   Catch him!

L C   Arrest him!

                (*Chase. Frantic but brief! Ad-libs sustain volume and energy.
                During chase* HARRY *frees* NUTS *from the cage, which opens as
                if by magic, with a flash, with one slice of the sword. At end
                of chase* HARRY *and* NUTS *are forced to hide in the Time-o-
                bile.* BRIAR ROSE *is too late to warn them not to shut the door.*
                KING, QUEEN, L C, NANNY, BRIAR ROSE, CEDRIC *and the* TIME
                FAIRY *assemble to see the Time-o-bile take off. The lights on
                stage dim as smoke and lights of the rising Time-o-bile take
                focus. Some backlighting leaves the characters in silhouette
                during the following brief vocal cacophony. Characters'
                overlapping reactions appropriate to the crisis as follows —
                these can be developed as necessary.*)

KING   He's got my magic sword! Come back! Elsie — don't just
                stand there! Do something!

QUEEN   Cuthbert — stop making an exhibition of yourself. Cuthbert
                — calm down!

BRIAR ROSE   Harry! Nuts! Don't leave me! Harry wait for me!

NANNY   Harry! My boy! Come back!

TIME FAIRY   My Time-o-bile! He's hijacked my Time-o-bile!

                (*Frontcloth in.*)

Scene Three

Frontcloth.

CARABOSSE   Curses! Foiled by a kitchen boy, no less.
Just for once, I'm in a bit of a mess.
Harry's got the sword — my back's against the wall:
I don't like it! I don't like it at all!
Alright — there's no need for you lot to gloat:
Your friend the princess is in the same boat.
She'll never see Harry again — how sad!
She'll have to marry Cedric now — too bad!
How I loathe her! Yes — and I hate you too —
Particularly when you hiss and boo!
I've only suffered a minor set-back:
Withdraw, regroup — then another attack.
I feel better already! Wait and see:
I'll be back — you've not heard the last from me!

(*Exit* CARABOSSE.)

L C   (*off right*) Briar Rose! Where are you?

(*Enter* BRIAR ROSE *from right, running.*)

QUEEN   (*off left*) Briar Rose!

BRIAR ROSE   (*stopping*) Oh no!

L C   }
CEDRIC   } (*off right*) Briar Rose!

QUEEN   }
KING   } (*off left*) Briar Rose!

BRIAR ROSE   I won't marry Cedric! I won't!

QUEEN   }
KING   } (*off left, fainter*) Where are you?

BRIAR ROSE   I'm sure Harry and Nuts didn't mean to fly off without me . . .

L C   }
CEDRIC   } (*off right*) Briar Rose!

BRIAR ROSE   (*to audience*) If anyone comes looking for me, you won't tell
them you've seen me, will you?

AUDIENCE   No!

BRIAR ROSE   Do you promise?

AUDIENCE   Yes!

L C   }   (*off right, closer*) Where are you?
CEDRIC

BRIAR ROSE   Thanks a lot!

     (*Exit* BRIAR ROSE, *left. Enter* CEDRIC *and* L C, *right.*)

CEDRIC   Briar Rose!

L C   Briar Rose!

BOTH   Where are you?

     (CEDRIC *turns and bumps into* L C. *Both fall.*)

L C   Doh!

CEDRIC   We could ask them if they've seen her.

L C   What? That rabble?

CEDRIC   It's worth a try.

L C   Oh, very well. (*To audience.*) Have you seen Briar Rose?

AUDIENCE   No!

CEDRIC   Are you sure?

AUDIENCE   Yes!

L C   Are you telling porkies?

AUDIENCE   No!

CEDRIC   Oh yes you are!

AUDIENCE   Oh no we're not!

L C   Oh yes you are!

AUDIENCE   Oh no we're not!

CEDRIC   Oh no you're not!

AUDIENCE   Oh yes we . . . (*Confusion.*)

CEDRIC   Ha, ha! Caught you!

L C   Doh! They don't know anything. Come along, Cedric.

             (*Exit L C, right.*)

L C   (*off, calling* BRIAR ROSE) Where are you?

CEDRIC   I'm here!

             (*Re-enter L C.*)

L C   Doh!

             (L C *cuffs* CEDRIC *and yanks him off. Enter* BRIAR ROSE, *left.*)

BRIAR ROSE   Thanks a lot! You were brilliant!

L C   (*off right, more distant*) Briar Rose!

BRIAR ROSE   But they're bound to find me eventually if I stay here. There
             are parts of the castle I've never explored. If I climb up to the
             highest tower I can live there all on my own till Harry comes
             back. I shall never give in. (*Strain of the Spinning Song —
             "Ah . . ."*) What beautiful singing. (*She listens.*) I wonder
             where it's coming from . . . ("Ah . . .") This way, I think.
             (*She moves left. Singing stops.*) It's stopped. (*Singing resumes
             from other side.*) No — it's coming from over here . . .

             (*Exit* BRIAR ROSE *right. Frontcloth out.*)

                              Scene Four

The Tower.

*Walled turreted area with central tower containing the spinning room at
the top, with steps curling round to door at the back (opening outwards).
Large windows all round are gauze, so old lady spinster (*CARABOSSE *in
benevolent disguise) is not initially visible.*

Silence as BRIAR ROSE *enters.*

BRIAR ROSE   I'm sure this is where the singing was coming from. It's a bit
             spooky up here — but I feel quite safe. I'm not frightened at
             all. (*Singing resumes.*) There it is again. It's coming from
             that tower . . .

(She climbs the steps tentatively. As she gets almost to the top, we bleed through the window-gauze to see the old spinster at her wheel. BRIAR ROSE *opens the door at the back and enters, apparently unnoticed by* CARABOSSE. *She listens.)*

*Number: Spinning Song (*CARABOSSE *and* BRIAR ROSE.*)*

CARABOSSE   THE SPINDLE TURNS —
SEE HOW THE THREAD GETS LONGER.
THE NEEDLE SHINES —
FEEL THE YARN GETTING STRONGER.
NOW YOU KNOW
HOW TO MAKE THE SILKEN THREAD GROW.

(Underscore continues below following:)

CARABOSSE   Welcome, my dear.

BRIAR ROSE   I'm sorry. I hope I didn't startle you.

CARABOSSE   Oh no, my dear. I've been expecting you.

BRIAR ROSE   Expecting me?

CARABOSSE   I've waited a long time.

BRIAR ROSE   I came as soon as I heard you sing.

CARABOSSE   I have often sung before.

BRIAR ROSE   I never heard you.

CARABOSSE   Perhaps it wasn't time for you to hear me.

(Pause.)

BRIAR ROSE   You sing so beautifully.

CARABOSSE   I used to *be* beautiful once, my dear. Just like you.

BRIAR ROSE   What are you doing?

CARABOSSE   I'm spinning.

BRIAR ROSE   Spinning?

CARABOSSE   The spinning wheel turns flax into thread, with which to sew. You guide the thread with your fingers — like this — and move the treadle with your foot.

BRIAR ROSE   May I have a go?

CARABOSSE   No!

(Music stops. She stops spinning.)

BRIAR ROSE   Why not? Please!

CARABOSSE   The needle is very sharp. There is an old legend. Should you prick your finger . . .

BRIAR ROSE   I shall be careful.

CARABOSSE   You must be very careful.

BRIAR ROSE   I promise.

CARABOSSE   Very well, but take great care.

(They change places. BRIAR ROSE *begins to spin. Music resumes. She is a natural. She begins to speed up.)*

BRIAR ROSE   THE SPINDLE TURNS —
CARABOSSE   SEE HOW THE THREAD GETS LONGER —

CARABOSSE   *(spoken)* Take care, my child. Take care.

BRIAR ROSE   THE NEEDLE SHINES —
CARABOSSE   FEEL THE YARN GETTING STRONGER.
NOW YOU KNOW —
BRIAR ROSE   NOW I KNOW

BOTH   NOW WE KNOW
HOW TO MAKE THE BEAUTIFUL, MAGICAL,
SILKEN THREAD GROW —

*(*BRIAR ROSE *pricks her finger. Underscore continues.)*

BRIAR ROSE   Ah! *(She stands.)* I've pricked my finger!

CARABOSSE   *(revealing herself)* Then die!

BRIAR ROSE   Help me! I feel faint!

CARABOSSE   Too late!
                Sixteen long years ago I sealed your fate.

BRIAR ROSE   Harry. (*She collapses.*)

CARABOSSE   At last — my triumph is complete!
                The wheel has come full circle. Oh — revenge is sweet!

                (*End underscore. Internal lighting down in spinning room.
                Gauze obscures* BRIAR ROSE (*and* CARABOSSE'S *exit.*) *General
                state up as* L C, CEDRIC *and* NANNY *enter.*)

L C   This way, your majesticality.

NANNY   I'm sure I heard voices.

                (*Enter* KING *and* QUEEN.)

KING   Well, Elsie?

QUEEN   Where's my Briar Rose?

NANNY   (*to audience*) Have you seen Briar Rose anywhere, dears?

AUDIENCE   Yes! (*Etc.*)

NANNY   Where?

                (*Tower glows.*)

AUDIENCE   Behind you!

                (*Tower stops glowing. They all look round and back again.*)

KING   I can't see her.

                (*Tower glows again.*)

AUDIENCE   Behind you!

                (*Tower stops glowing. They all look round and back again.*)

NANNY   Stop playing tricks, you naughty lot.

                (*Tower glows again and remains lit.*)

AUDIENCE   Behind you!

(They all look again.)

NANNY   You were right.

QUEEN   And there's Briar Rose!

KING   Having a little doze.

ALL   Ahh!

L C   And look — there's a spinning wheel.

NANNY   A spinning wheel! My word — I haven't seen one of them for
             at least sixteen years.

ALL   *(casually)* No . . . *(Suddenly clock.)* A spinning wheel!

             (They run for the steps to the tower QUEEN *first, followed by*
             KING.*)*

QUEEN   Briar Rose.

NANNY   My baby . . .

             *(CARABOSSE appears on the top step and stops them in their
             tracks.)*

CARABOSSE   Not so fast! How pathetic can you get?
             You thought you'd heard the last of me — and yet
             I've been watching you — biding my time —
             Waiting till Briar Rose was in her prime.
             Sweet sixteen — lively, generous and free.
             Having a doze! Hah! She looks dead to me.
             Past hope — past grief: now no one can save her.

QUEEN   There was talk of a prince —

CARABOSSE   Do me a favour!
             That Time Fairy's well past her sell-by date.
             As godmothers go — deeply second-rate.
             Well: Tempus Fugit, as the Romans say.
             I'll be getting along. Have a vile day!

             (Exit CARABOSSE.)

KING   I don't believe it. Elsie — this is all your fault.

QUEEN   Oh, Cuthbert — don't start all over again. It's everybody's
             fault or it's nobody's fault. Briar Rose is dead. Nothing else
             matters now.

             (*Enter* TIME FAIRY.)

TIME FAIRY   Well said: but you're mistaken in your grief.
             Briar Rose is not dead. Look: I'll be brief.
             She sleeps. When she wakes, as I foretold —

KING   She'll be one hundred and sixteen years old!
             That's a fat lot of use. We'll all be dead
             By the time she wakes up. (*To* QUEEN.) That's what you said
             After the christening —

QUEEN   Cuthbert!

KING   Yes, dear?

QUEEN   Be quiet, precious, or you'll get a thick ear!

TIME FAIRY   If you consent — I'll put you to sleep too.
             What do you say?

NANNY   Sounds too good to be true!
             While she kips for a century, safe and sound —

L C   We'll be zizzing too —

TIME FAIRY   So, when she comes round,
             Woken at last by a prince —

QUEEN   With a kiss!

TIME FAIRY   No one will be alone.

CEDRIC   Hang on! I'd miss
             Twenty six thousand episodes of Home and Away:
             That's quite a consideration, I have to say.

KING   All those in favour —

ALL   (*except* CEDRIC) Ay!

L C   (*stern*) Cedric!

CEDRIC   (*reluctant*) Ay!

NANNY   What fun!

QUEEN   (*impatient*) Come on, then!

TIME FAIRY   No sooner said . . .
             (*She puts them all to sleep in turn.*) . . . than done!

             (*Gauze slowly in over following few lines.*)

             The clock starts now. One hundred years to go.
             The docks begin to sprout — the weeds to grow.
             Ivy, creeper, lilac and the wild vine —
             Sweet willow and the sleepy eglantine.

             (*Gauze in.* TIME FAIRY *continues from the side as gauze is
             frontlit with forest projection.*)

                              Scene Five

Gauze: frontlit with forest/briars.

The action is continuous from Scene Four.

TIME FAIRY   Slim elder, spindle, birch with silver cloak;
             Tall pine, strong sycamore and sturdy oak.
             Dead to the world — King Cuthbert and his queen,
             Shaded by the luscious evergreen,
             Sleep sound. Protect them, spirits, as they doze:
             Nanny, Elsie, Princess Briar Rose —
             Even the dreadful Cedric, I suppose —
             Safe and secure, the higher the forest grows.
             So, let them travel on Time's silken wings,
             Dreaming those dreams that only sweet slumber brings.

             (*Enter* CARABOSSE.)

CARABOSSE   Sentimental clap-trap! I've had enough.
             From now on, midget, the going gets tough.
             Your precious forest will grow rank and coarse:
             With deadly nightshade, blackthorn, briars and gorse.
             So thick, so tangled will these brambles grow
             That any prince who seeks to have a go
             At getting in will suffocate and die.
             I rather hope that one or two might try!

TIME FAIRY   You don't mean to tell me that you intend
             To hand around here till these hundred years end?

CARABOSSE   Yes — that's exactly what I plan to do.
            But that doesn't mean that you have to too!

TIME FAIRY No choice. I'm the victim of a hijack:
            Can't move on till I get my Time-o-bile back.

CARABOSSE   When will that be?

TIME FAIRY   In a hundred years' time.

CARABOSSE   I'm staying put!

TIME FAIRY   You'll be well past your prime.

CARABOSSE   Tough.

TIME FAIRY   You said it!

CARABOSSE   Miaow!

TIME FAIRY   Looks like we're stuck.

BOTH   Together! For the next hundred years! Yuk!

            Number: 100 Years With You (TIME FAIRY/CARABOSSE)

CARABOSSE   I COULD BE TRAPPED IN A LIFT WITH A RATTLESNAKE,
            OR STUNG BY A SWARM OF BEES;
            DISCOVER A SLUG IN MY BIRTHDAY CAKE —
            OR FIND THAT I'D GOT FLEAS.
            I COULD FALL HEADLONG INTO A COWPAT,
            AND BE COVERED IN SLIME AND GOO.
            BUT THE WORST THING OF ALL WOULD BE
            TO SPEND A HUNDRED YEARS WITH YOU!

TIME FAIRY I COULD BE CAPTURED BY BANDITS, FORCED TO THE
                                                    GROUND,
            TIED TO A RAILWAY LINE.
            I'D HEAR THE TRAIN APPROACHING,
            SENDING SHIVERS UP MY SPINE.
            BUT I WOULDN'T BE SCARED — I'D WAVE AND SMILE,
            AND HOLLER — "TOODLE-OO!"
            'COS I'D RATHER BE RUN OVER BY A 125
            THAN SPEND A HUNDRED YEARS WITH YOU!

CARABOSSE   PERHAPS I'LL USE MY MAGIC POWERS
            AND TURN HER INTO A TOAD.
            OH WHAT FUN TO HEAR HER CROAK

AS SHE HOPS OFF DOWN THE ROAD.

TIME FAIRY I'LL CLICK MY FINGERS, CAST A SPELL
AND THEN, WITH ANY LUCK —
THE NEXT SHE KNOWS SHE'LL BE WADDLING AROUND,
QUACKING LIKE DONALD DUCK!

BOTH I'LL USE EVERY SCHEME, EVERY TRICK,
THERE'S NOTHING I WON'T DO.
FOR I'D RATHER DIE THAN SPEND
ANOTHER MINUTE WITH YOU.

TIME FAIRY I COULD BE BURIED ALIVE IN A DUNGEON,
OR THROWN INTO A PIT —

CARABOSSE I COULD BE BOILED IN OIL, FRIED IN FAT,
OR ROASTED ON A SPIT.

BOTH BUT THERE ISN'T A SINGLE TORTURE
THAT YOU COULD PUT ME THROUGH,
THAT WOULD BE HALF AS HORRID AS SPENDING
A HUNDRED YEARS WITH YOU.

(*Lose front projection and bleed through gauze to the overgrown tower.*)

TIME FAIRY TIME HAS PASSED —
CARABOSSE   THE BRIARS HAVE GROWN —
BOTH THE HUNDRED YEARS ARE THROUGH.
CARABOSSE AND GUESS WHAT —
TIME FAIRY I'M STILL HERE —
CARABOSSE AND EVEN WORSE —
TIME FAIRY EVEN WORSE —
CARABOSSE EVEN WORSE —

BOTH You are too!

(*Exit* TIME FAIRY *and* CARABOSSE. *Gauze out.*)

Scene Six

The overgrown Tower.

The sleeping figures should be almost completely concealed by brambles/ briars, etc, as should be much of the tower itself.

As the gauze flies out, three Bramble Bogwoppits — GIRLS 1, 2 and 3 — emerge as if from the undergrowth and come forward.

Brief dance of the Bramble Bogwoppits.

HARRY   (*coming through audience*) Come on, Nuts!

             (*The Bogwoppits scamper off.*)

HARRY   Nuts! Where are you?

             (*Enter* NUTS *from the other side of the auditorium, wearing a small sword, a less 'magic'-looking replica of* HARRY'S. NUTS *can have fun with audience on the way down, eg, steal a sweet, run along a row — in the unlikely extent of a sparse house — etc. Some ad-libbing from* HARRY *may be needed.*)

             (*once on stage*) Come on. Stop monkeying around. I've had a funny feeling about today — ever since we disembarked from the Time-o-bile. It's over a hundred years since we left home, Nuts. I can hardly believe it. What adventures we've had — eh, Nuts?

             Number: Prince's Song. Solo (HARRY), *but musically a reprise of the* BRIAR ROSE/HARRY *duet from Act One*

HARRY   WE FLEW INTO THE FUTURE,
             WE TRAVELLED FAR AND WIDE.
             WE HITCHED A LIFT ON A SHOOTING STAR,
             TOOK A MAGIC CARPET RIDE.

             WE CAUGHT A ROCKET TO THE MOON,
             AND THAT WAS HOW WE FOUND
             THE WORLD WAS SHAPED LIKE A BALLOON —
             YES, FOLKS, IT WAS ROUND!
             CHRISTOPHER COLUMBUS
             HAD NOTHING ON US!

             THERE WERE SO MANY PLACES IN THE WORLD,
             THINGS TO SEE AND DO.
             IT WAS TIME FOR AN ADVENTURE —
             ME AND YOU!

             WE ROWED ACROSS THE ATLANTIC,
             WE PADDLED UP THE NILE.
             WE FISHED FOR SHARKS IN A BLUE LAGOON,
             CAPTURED A CROCODILE.

WE CROSSED THE ALPS WITH HANNIBAL,
PLAYED BOWLS WITH FRANCIS DRAKE,
HELPED PAINT THE SISTINE CHAPEL,
THAT WAS A LUCKY BREAK!
MICHELANGELO
JUST SAID: "HAVE A GO!"

SO PACK YOUR BAGS,
BOOK THE TICKET —
THUMB A LIFT,
TAKE THE TRAIN.
RIDE A CAMEL,
OR A HORSE,
CATCH THE BUS,
OR AN AEROPLANE.
JUST GO!

(*Underscore continues over speech.*)

I feel as if I've been on a kind of Royal Tour. I feel . . . well, I
don't feel a hundred years old, that's for sure.

(NUTS *is getting excited. He is ahead of the game and is
pointing to the tower. Perhaps he tries to get through, and
can't.*)

What's the matter, Nuts? You don't want to go that way —
it's all overgrown.

(*The spinning room starts to glow dimly through the briars.*)

Hang on, I can see a light!

(NUTS *is frantic, and hacking ineffectually with his sword.*)

Alright, calm down! Calm down! Let me have a go.

(*He takes his sword. He hacks three times. On the third hack,
as if by magic, the upper section of the brambles/undergrowth
flies out, revealing the upper part of the tower. The spinning
room has faded.*)

I know where we are now, Nuts. This is the top of the castle.
We're home.

(*Meanwhile* NUTS *is getting frantic. He takes* HARRY'S *sword
and tries vainly to hack through the main barrier of
brambles.*)

Alright, alright. Give me the sword.

(*He takes the sword. Three more hacks. The main portion of the brambles flies out. The sleeping figures are now revealed. There should be a clear path up the tower steps. Some of the undergrowth/brambles, however, should remain — so as not to give the impression that the whole of the forest has disappeared at a stroke! Underscore stops. Silence.*)

Ma! I don't believe it! Surely she . . . (NUTS *mimes sleep.*) Asleep? But how . . . ? Ma, wake up! Elsie! Cedric . . . ! Wake up!

(*He can't wake them. The* KING *snores loudly.*)

The king and queen! Fast asleep too! Your majesties, wake up!

(*The tower glows more strongly than before.* NUTS *draws* HARRY'S *attention to it.*)

It's Briar Rose! Princess! Princess!

(HARRY *goes up the steps leaving his sword at the top. He goes into the spinning room. Silence.*)

Wake up, princess. (*Kiss.*) Wake up! (BRIAR ROSE *awakes.*)

BRIAR ROSE   Harry! I was just dreaming about you! I feel so sleepy. I don't remember . . . didn't you fly away . . . and Nuts?

HARRY   It's alright. We're here. And so are the king and queen. They've been asleep too —

(BRIAR ROSE *runs out to the top of the stairs, and comes down to kiss the* QUEEN.)

BRIAR ROSE   Mama! Mama! (*Kiss.*) Wake up!

QUEEN   (*waking up*) Ah — Briar Rose, there you are. We've been looking for you everywhere. Cuthbert! (*Kiss.*) Wake up!

KING   (*waking up*) What's the time? I must have dropped off. What's the time?

QUEEN   Time for another kiss, Bertie-poo!

KING   Ooh — Esme!

                (BRIAR ROSE *sees* NUTS, *who jumps into her arms.*)

BRIAR ROSE   Nuts!

                (HARRY *has gone over to* NANNY *and* L C.)

HARRY   Ma! (*Kiss.*) Wake up!

NANNY   (*waking up*) Harry! My boy! You've come home! Where's
                Elsie? I want Elsie. (*She sees him.*) Elsie! (*Kiss.*) Wake up.

L C   (*waking up*) My Nanny! My little Nanny Fanny Annie. (*He
                returns her kisses energetically.*)

NANNY   Oooh! Your kisses are something else!

L C   Don't call me 'Something Else'!

HARRY   Cedric! Who's going to wake him up?

                (*All are dubious.* L C *is about to, but* NUTS *intervenes and
                kisses* CEDRIC.)

ALL   Ahh!

                (CEDRIC *wakes up, clearly having a nightmare.*)

CEDRIC   Aaaarrhh! Let me out! Let me out! (*Awake now.*) Oh! I dreamt
                I was in this horrible cage. And Carabosse came to chop my
                head off and — (*He sees* NUTS *and smiles.*) Oh! Hello, Nuts!

KING   Carabosse. Carabosse. That name rings a bell.
                Always cross, I recall —

QUEEN   Yes — she put a spell
                On Briar Rose. It's all coming back now.

L C   A nasty piece of work.

NANNY   Yes — a right cow!

                (*Enter* CARABOSSE *at top of the steps.*)

CARABOSSE   You fools!

BRIAR ROSE   She's got the sword!

CARABOSSE   Prepare to die!
Say your prayers. One by one. The end is nigh.
Well, Harry. What a silly oversight
To drop your sword. So — who's the first to fight?

KING   I would be, but . . . I'm a bit out of breath.

CARABOSSE   Coward! (*She freezes him and his group.*)

HARRY   I'll fight you.

CARABOSSE   Come on, then. To the death.

(*They fight.* NUTS *and* CEDRIC *also involved.* NANNY, L C *and*
CEDRIC *can also be 'frozen' during fight.* HARRY *manages to
retrieve the sword.* CARABOSSE *is defeated.*)

CARABOSSE   Spare me!

ALL   Hurrah!

CARABOSSE   I promise to be good — I swear!

NANNY   Don't you believe it, dears. She's all hot air.

CARABOSSE   I know I've been wicked. Nevertheless,
Invite me to the wedding of the prince and princess
And I'll never ever be wicked again.

KING   Hang on a minute: it's perfectly plain
I've missed the point here. What prince? That's Harry.
And I'm certainly not letting him marry
My daughter.

BRIAR ROSE   But he woke me with a kiss:
He must be a prince!

QUEEN   He can't be!

NANNY   He is!

KING   Eh?

NANNY   Many years ago, over a hundred to be imprecise, there was a
terrible battle, and King Henry the Good was defeated,
leaving his baby son, little Prince Hal —

KING   *Don't mention the prince!*

QUEEN   (*sweetly*) Bertie!

NANNY   I was up the front doing my bit for the troops. I rescued him from the field of battle and brought him up to live with me as my own son —

HARRY   Ma . . . ?

NANNY   (*deep curtsey*) Your majesticals!

HARRY   Ma!

NANNY   Harry! (*Big hug.*)

KING   Elsie — I've made a decision.

L C   (*impressed*) Well done, your majesticality!

KING   Time marches on. Now I'm a hundred and forty ummmm . . . years old, I can't run about fighting battles any more. Must look after the old ticker, don't you know. Harry, er . . . your highness: you can keep the magic sword.

HARRY   Thank you, your majesty.

KING   And seeing you're a prince after all, you *may* marry my daughter. How about that?

HARRY   I'm honoured, your majesty.

NANNY   (*aside*) Lovely manners!

HARRY   If Briar Rose consents.

NANNY   (*aside*) It's all in the upbringing, of course.

KING   She'd better consent!

QUEEN   Bertie!

BRIAR ROSE I consent with all my heart.

KING   I should jolly well think so too.

CEDRIC   Three cheers for Prince Hal! Hip-hip —

ALL   Hurray!

CEDRIC   Hip-hip —

ALL   Hurray!

CEDRIC   Hip-hip —

ALL   HURRAY!!

(*Frontcloth in.*)

Scene Seven

Frontcloth — including songsheet.

Enter TIME FAIRY.

TIME FAIRY   I'm in danger of losing my mind!
             I nipped off — came back: what do I find?
             Harry has turned into Prince Hal,
             Nuts has become Cedric's best pal,
             Cuthbert's battle-ardour's flagging,
             Esmeralda's stopped her nagging,
             Elsie's in love and then — oh brother!
             Nanny's set to become Queen Mother!
             Carabosse is everybody's friend.
             Where, I ask you, will it all end?
             I feel like calling it a day.
             'Time, the Great Healer' — yes, OK —
             But right now, folks, my chief requirement
             Is a nice, quiet, early retirement.
             My Time-o-bile's ready. I think I'll fly —
             After the wedding. Cheeri-bye!

             (*Exit* TIME FAIRY. *Enter* NANNY.)

NANNY   Hello, dears!

AUDIENCE   Hello, Nanny Fanny Annie!

             Songsheet. (NANNY, L C *and audience.*)

             CLEAN YOUR TEETH,
             BRUSH YOUR HAIR.
             CHANGE YOUR DIRTY UNDERWEAR.
             SCRUB YOUR FEET BETWEEN YOUR TOES,

BLOW THE BOGIES DOWN YOUR NOSE.
ALL THE BITS YOU HAVEN'T DONE FOR YEARS.
AND DON'T FORGET TO WASH BEHIND YOUR EARS!

(Dialogue for this scene may be improvised or scripted as the actors prefer. Suggested sequence as follows.)

NANNY *announces to the audience that they are all invited to the Royal Wedding, but they need smartening up. So she'll teach them a cleansing song.*

She wants L C's *help but he's got a bit shy since they became an 'item'. Audience helps call "Elsie".*

L C *and* NANNY *sing the song. Invite audience to join. They don't know the words. Words descend.*

NANNY *notes not many grown-ups doing the actions. Bring on* GIRL 2 *and* BOY 2 *to help.*

Sing again with actions. Then competition. Grown-ups first. (Led by L C.) *Then kids. (Led by* NANNY *and children.)*

Maestro judges. Kids win. (Just.) Exit children.

Sing through one last time at double speed.

(Exit NANNY *and* L C. *Frontcloth out.)*

Scene Eight

The Royal Hall. (Walkdown.)

Decked out for the wedding. Banners, bunting, streamers, etc.

A brief formal dance with the children. Enter TIME FAIRY.

TIME FAIRY   Our panto, friends, is drawing to a close:
Today's the wedding day of Briar Rose.
This time, everybody's invited —
Including Carabosse —

(Enter CARABOSSE.)

CARABOSSE   I'm that excited!
I love being nice — strange as that may seem.
And it's done wonders for my self-esteem.

TIME FAIRY   That's it for now — I have to fly.
             I take my bow —

CARABOSSE   And so do I.

(*They bow and split to the sides. Walkdown as follows:* CEDRIC
and NUTS *bow and split to R and L.* QUEEN *and* KING *bow and
break R.* NANNY *and* L C *bow and break L.* BRIAR ROSE *and*
HARRY *bow and stay centre.*)

BRIAR ROSE   Welcome to our wedding, friends!

KING   I'd like to say —

HARRY   Welcome!

KING   — a few words on this happy day.

QUEEN   Bertie, don't get pompous, there's a poppet.

KING   As father of the bride —

QUEEN   (*firmly*) Bertie, stop it!
             I fancy a dance. Nanny — what do you say?

NANNY   I'm game if you are, dear! Elsie?

L C   OK.

QUEEN   Ready when you are, Maestro!

ALL   Take it away!

Celebration: Life is a Bowl of Cherries (*reprise*) — (*Finale*
— FULL COMPANY.)

ALL   NO MORE HANGING AROUND —
             WE'VE GOT OUR FEET FIRMLY ON THE GROUND,
             AND OUR HEAD IN THE CLOUDS,
             WE'RE SO PROUD:
             LIFE IS A BOWL OF CHERRIES!

             WE'RE ALL GATHERED HERE
             FOR THE WEDDING OF THE YEAR.
             WE'RE FEELING GREAT
             SO LET'S CELEBRATE:

LIFE IS A BOWL OF CHERRIES!

(*Dance break.*)

WE'VE ALL HAD A BALL,
THANKS FOR COMING ONE AND ALL.
SEE YOU SOON! IT'S TIME TO GO!
MERRY CHRISTMAS! (HAPPY NEW YEAR!) CHEERIO!

(*Waving, final bows. Frontcloth in. Playout.*)